The New Apartment
SMART LIVING IN SMALL SPACES

The New Apartment

SMART LIVING IN SMALL SPACES

Montse Borràs

Universe

First published in the United States of America in 2007
by UNIVERSE PUBLISHING
A Division of Rizzoli International Publications, Inc.
300 Park Avenue South
New York, NY 10010
www.rizzoliusa.com

Originally published in Spain in 2007 as *Nuevos pequeños espacios urbanos*
by Loft Publications S.L.
© 2007 Loft Publications S.L.
Via Laietana 32, 4° Of. 92
08003 Barcelona, Spain
Tel.: +34 932 688 088
Fax: +34 932 687 073
loft@loftpublications.com
www.loftpublications.com

2007 2008 2009 2010 / 10 9 8 7 6 5 4 3 2 1

Printed in Spain by Anman Gràfiques del Vallès

ISBN-10: 0-7893-1529-7
ISBN-13: 978-0-7893-1529-8

Library of Congress Control Number: 2006907915

Editor: Montse Borràs

Editor in Chief: Catherine Collin

Art Director: Mireia Casanovas Soley

Graphic design and Layout: Anabel Naranjo

Translation: Bridget Vranckx, Ana Cañizares, Julia Hendler, Jay Noden

Front cover photo © Jacques Dirand
Back cover photo © Angel Baltanás

CONTENTS

8
Open Space
Solutions

10
Mini Loft in Paris

16
Apartment in
Gramercy Park

24
Apartment in
Via Belsito

32
DT Loft

38
Apartment on
Almirante Street

44
Stables on
Ridge Street 1

52
Loft 108

58
Loft in Blanes

66
Attic in Chueca

72
McGrath Loft

78
C.E.D.V. House

84
Apartment in
Classical Madrid

90
Apartment in
El Born

96
Raper Apartment

104
Apartment in
Sant Feliu

110
Apartment on
Rue St. Fiacre

116
Joralemon
Street Loft

122
Ronda Loft

128
LU.DOmus

134
Studio on
Thompson Street

140
Residence for a
Designer

148
Apartment on
Rue Rivoli

154
Apartment in an
Industrial Building

158
Apartment in
West Village

164
Apartment in
São Paulo

170
Apartment in
the West End

176
Loft on
Las Minas Street

185
Multiple Level
Solutions

186
Vandekerkhove-
Roelens House

190
House HP

196
Mini Loft
in Rome

202
Mezzanine on Top
of a Wardrobe

208
Apartment in
Brasilia

216
Lofts in
Glorieta de Quevedo

222
Apartment for a Musician

228
Vila Grandela

234
Studio on Escorial Street

240
Apartment in Buenos Aires

246
House in the Center of Ghent

252
Darlinghurst Apartment

260
Duplex in Malasaña

268
Apartment in Attic

276
Duplex in Greeenwich Village

284
Little Fisherman's House

290
Studio on Madison Avenue

296
Smart Solutions

298
Carlton Ramsey Apartment

306
Perraton Apartment

312
Small Industrial Apartment

318
Player's Pad

326
Bayswater Apartment

334
Interior Cabins

340
Apartment on the Atlantic Coast

344
Enric Rovira Apartment

352
Apartment on Rue Cadet

358
Apartment near the Colosseum

364
Morrell Apartment

372
Pied à terre in Paris

378
Day Freckman Apartment

386
Heart of Home

390
Ponzano House

396
Mark and Avi's Apartment

403
Transportable Solutions

404
Nomad Home

408
Self-sufficient Modules

412
Loftcube

418
Intelligent House

INTRODUCTION

It is a well-known fact that it is possible to live in the smallest of spaces. In fact, it is becoming more and more common to lead an independent lifestyle, alone or as a couple, in a space of small dimensions, especially if you want to live in the center of a large city. New, affordable housing developments maximize space reduction, designed for one or two people who spend most of the day out of the house. Real estate prices in urban centers or the high cost of renovating old, bigger apartments, which till recently was the main alternative, make it increasingly difficult for people to obtain their own space. If we add to this the transitory nature of our first homes as independent adults and the urgency there is to possess an individualized space that suits our needs and tastes, it seems logical that today's urbanite is likely to set up home in increasingly small spaces.

It is fascinating to observe how most new trends, once established and accepted, transform and acquire new and more complex dimensions and are adopted by different social and cultural strata. Consider, for example, hip-hop, yoga, or the bicycle as a mode of urban transport.

Miniscule, modern, and multipurpose apartments, which have been common in large Asian metropolises since the years following the Second World War, were until recently quite shocking to us. They seemed alienating, the definitive end to a type of hedonism to which we all aspire. However, in just a few years the concept of the small apartment has transformed and become a symbol of modernity in western cities, adopted by larger and larger segments of society. Technological advances have, without doubt, contributed to this change, both in materials and equipment. The fact that a single room can offer different functions has become a luxury when done using innovative materials and ultramodern technology. Making the most of the space, taking advantage of every inch of an apartment, both on horizontal surfaces and on wall and even ceiling surfaces (for example, installing rails for hanging the television) has become a challenge. Aesthetic tendencies have followed suit, and this exploration can develop now more than ever with the use of textures and colors that recover the essential, playful appearance in interior design: plastics of a thousand different shapes and colors, pieces of wood that curve, or bold lighting. The furious minimalism has disappeared, giving way to new styles, but it has left, as a legacy, the taste for what is essential and for free spaces.

This book illustrates the latest tendencies regarding the design of small homes, using highly diverse styles and also more timeless formulas, but always from an inventive and intuitive point of view. It features compact apartments like small boxes or vertebrae stretching towards the sky, spaces that have shed their previous skin or are amplified by reflecting the light and the space using mirrors and shiny textures, and a glance at a future that has already arrived: small, prefabricated spaces, which are both flexible and transportable. This is a path which is being fearlessly explored, a tendency which is building up to be a very possible way of life for not-so-distant future generations.

OPEN SPACE SOLUTIONS

Mini Loft in Paris

Philippe Harden

Paris, France, 2006

This apartment was previously divided into a succession of small rooms. A long and narrow floor plan free of structural walls made it possible to create an open-plan space that emphasized the apartment's most distinctive features. Similar to country houses, the apartment is entered through the kitchen, conceived as another living space that communicates with the living and dining areas. An eating area was placed at an angle, creating an intimate corner that received abundant daylight. The removal of all partitions allowed for uninterrupted views of the row of windows that occupy the main facade, through which the patio of the building can be accessed. The side of the apartment without any windows accommodates the library, working studio, bathroom, and common areas. A freestanding partition comprised of two closets serves to separate visually the living area from the bedroom. The bathroom was conceived as a prolongation of the bedroom, which maintains the sanitary space out of sight. The kitchen and bathroom surfaces were covered with blue stone from Belgium. The design solutions employed achieve an intimacy between different areas within a continuous space.

615 sq ft

Photographs © **Jacques Dirand**

The kitchen and dining areas have been set on a wooden platform, which creates a subtle separation from the living room. The little corner by the main entrance is used as a casual breakfast space.

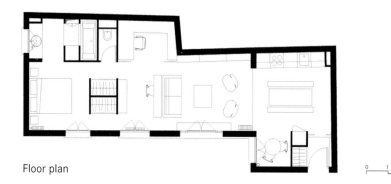

Floor plan

Apartment in Gramercy Park

Page Goolrick

New York, USA, 2005

600 sq ft

Photographs © **John M. Hall**

The designer Page Goolrick acquired this small apartment in an elegant 1950s building with the goal of converting it into her own pied-à-terre in Manhattan. The challenge was to create a flexible and comfortable space that was both minimal and intimate. All interior divisions were eliminated—with the exception of the bathroom—and folding glass panels were fixed onto steel rails to separate the different areas. Many of the furniture pieces were made-to-measure, such as the folding office desk designed to accommodate the precise width occupied by a laptop, printer, and notebook. The kitchen, located between the entrance and the living room, is hidden behind translucent sliding panels, as is the bedroom, in which a rotating device allows the flat screen TV to be viewed from practically anywhere in the apartment. Despite its reduced surface area, the kitchen offers plenty of cooking space, the dining area can seat up to six people, and the entrance hall integrates ample storage area. Thanks to the new configuration, spaces can be transformed according to the needs of the tenant with solutions that are both flexible and economic.

Every last detail of this small New York apartment has been designed and built to make the most of the light and the space.

Movable panes can create two different apartments. When the glass panes have been moved back, the bedroom and living room become one space, and the television can be turned to be viewed from the living room.

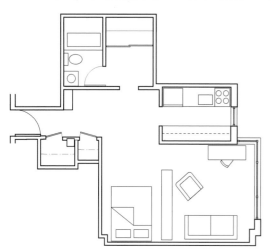

Exisiting floor plan

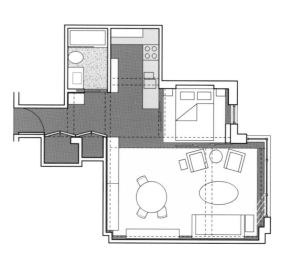

New floor plan

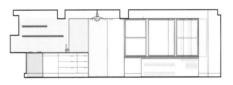

Translucent layers - West section

Opaque layers - South section

Spatial layers - East section

Apartment in Via Belsito

Vittorio Notari & Laura Manzini

Naples, Italy, 2005

This apartment is part of a renovation carried out on the last two floors of a splendid building near the Bay of Naples. The small penthouse enjoys stunning views of the Mediterranean Sea and receives abundant natural light throughout the day. The aim of introducing as much light as possible led to the creation of an open-plan lay-out in the style of Le Corbusier. The structure of the space, as well as its surrounding landscape and the materials used, give the residence a timeless environment. A curved wall that stops short of the ceiling encloses the bathroom with-out preventing the passage of light. Similarly, the storage unit between the kitchen and living room serves to separate each area while linking them at the same time. A small breakfast area incorporates a curtain that can be pulled to con-ceal the sink for a more minimalist effect. The curved bathroom features a shower and toilet contained within two independent cubicles of translucent glass. A dressing room between the bedroom and living room makes for an unclut-tered environment. A panel that doubles as a headboard separates the studio from the bed-room, which offers mesmerizing views of the sea and the horizon.

700 sq ft

Photographs © **Paolo Utimpergher**

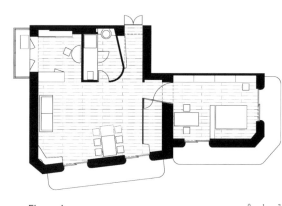

Floor plan

0 1 2

All the doorframes have been removed, and the connections between the rooms are open, becoming cleancut thresholds, as opposed to the round walls that enclose the bathroom.

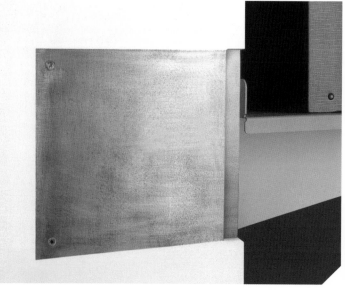

A massive wooden wardrobe was built on the wall that divides the two main rooms, creating a visual and atmospheric distance between them.

DT Loft

Mandi Rafaty/Tag Front

Los Angeles, California, 2005

The goal of the design of this apartment in the heart of Los Angeles was to organize all of the elements in such a way to make the space seem larger than its actual size. This was achieved through a system of rail-suspended steel and wood platforms that slide back and forth to provide privacy where needed without visually interrupting the space. A curtain with steel rods gives an intimate atmosphere to the bedroom by allowing light and views to filter through. The architect designed all of the furnishings for the apartment. The platforms that supports the bed and closet, as well as the tables and kitchen elements, all benefit from the abundance of light. A dining table with an incorporated storage space was set up as a divider between the kitchen and living room. A custom-made steel unit placed horizontally along the wall adjacent to the windows contains all electrical and audiovisual equipments and also holds a clever and elegant storage system for compact discs.

590 sq ft

Photographs © **Dean Pappas/Tag Front**

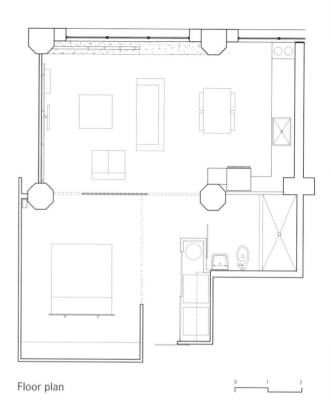

Floor plan

Partitions were designed using different materials and textures, allowing a playful interaction. A horizontal steel rail on the side wall integrates all the music and television equipments.

The aim of this project was to create an efficient loft that felt open and roomier than the actual square footage would allow. It had to include a full-sized kitchen, bathroom, laundry area, living area, and bedroom in a very limited space.

Apartment on Almirante Street

CGR Arquitectos

Madrid, Spain, 2005

750 sq ft

Photographs © **Ángel Baltanás/Carmen Baudín (Stylist)**

The remodeling of this apartment began with a very limited budget in terms of both construction and interior design. Luckily, the apartment had abundant light on both sides. First of all, the architects decided to bring all daytime activities into one room. To clearly distinguish the activities, the living room was placed next to the balcony, making the most of the light, and the kitchen was built in the room's inner corner with the window leading to one of the interior patios. All areas are opened by a pressure system to avoid the need for handles and allow the walls to merge. Meanwhile, two cast-iron columns painted in white, located between the kitchen and living room, are a reference to the home's past, and the supporting beams remain exposed. Pinewood planks, covered in glossy varnish, are used as flooring throughout the apartment.

The headboard in the bedroom is a small raised wall, which hides a small work space, and allows the same desk lamp to be used for work and for nighttime reading. Here, there is again an uniformity in the choice of materials in order to increase visually the sense of space.

This apartment enjoys plenty of natural light thanks to balconies on either side. The living room, dining room, and kitchen were grouped into one room, with original cast-iron pillars painted in white.

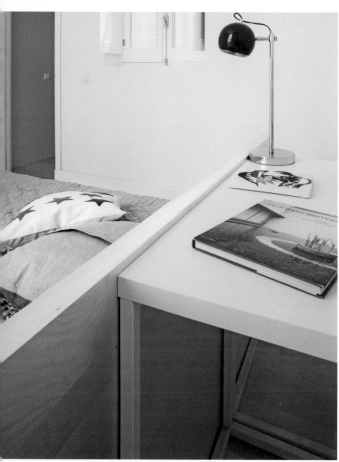

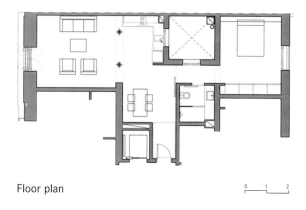

Floor plan

0 1 2

Stables on Ridge Street 1

William Smart/Smart Design Studio

Surry Hills, Australia, 2004

376 sq ft

Photographs © **Sharrin Rees**

Located in a legendary building in Sydney, these stables were nearly destroyed by a fire before being converted into artists' studios during the last few decades. They were recently renovated into contemporary residences, which preserve the original characteristics of the building. Layers of plaster were removed from the walls, revealing the crafted detail of the underlying surfaces. Oxidized areas were substituted with galvanized steel, and the staircase that envelops the common areas was restored. The ground floor was converted into a working studio, designating the upper floor as a small apartment. A simple layout makes for a highly versatile and flexible space. The kitchen and bathroom are perceived as white inserts that contrast with the rough materials of the ceiling, walls, and floors, and located against a wall to create as much free space as possible. The dining table separates the living room from the kitchen, which is comprised of a single unit that contains all the appliances and storage areas. Spotlights highlight specific areas, emphasizing the geometry created by the inclined beams and triangular windows.

These former stables have been converted into a flexible space, which can be adapted to a living and/or work environment, with an office downstairs and a living area upstairs.

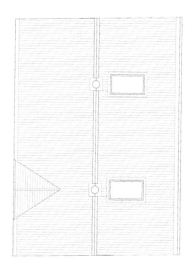

Roof plan

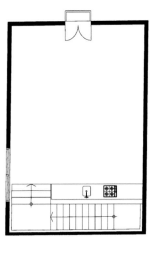

Floor plan

0   1   2

Loft 108

Anne Bugugnani

Barcelona, Spain, 2002

690 sq ft

The remodeling of this home is based on the selection and application of materials that provide comfort on one hand and organize the space in different, distinct functions on the other. The fact that the apartment only receives daylight on one side has worked to its advantage in the creation of fluid spaces and semi-closed areas. To create a unique entrance hall, a long white curtain hides the door and creates a moving drawing. At the same time, an L-shaped partition wall, which starts at the entrance and hides a built-in closet, shelters the bedroom. A continuous rectangular opening in the partition wall's two segments allows light to penetrate to the end, while establishing a visual continuity from the entrance to the apartment's extreme opposite. The bathroom, totally open to the exterior, is located next to the bedroom, so that the partition wall, which serves as the shower cabin, is also a headboard. The bathroom fittings are hidden behind an L-shaped wall that is erected as a background for the open kitchen and hides electrical appliances and the kitchen sink. A studio was created in a small corner, with an inclined drawing table and a desk, which leans against a part of the wall that is painted in blackboard paint to scribble notes. The rest of the space, full of light, is for relaxation, reading, and social occasions.

This sun-filled space is organizad into sections with different functions. An L-shaped partition wall hides a closet, while a small corner has been decked out as a studio.

Loft in Blanes

Ferran Galvany/Lofts Bcn Disseny

Blanes, Spain, 2006

700 sq ft

Photographs © **Óscar Gutiérrez**

An old office space in the center of Blanes on the Costa Brava was entirely gutted out and transformed into a residence. The designers, specialized in creating diaphanous structures, encountered an elongated floor plan measuring over fifty-two feet long and thirteen feet wide with only one source of natural light. Distinct divisions were created to define the different spaces. The bedroom is separated from the living room by a partition that occupies very little space to maintain fluidity. A glass panel was introduced between the bedroom and the bathroom, placing the shower behind a translucent glass wall to maintain privacy as well as the infiltration of light. An island structure defines the kitchen area, separating it from the living room and the dining table located in front. Local materials such as porcelain and terrazzo were used for the bathroom and floors, while chromatic arrangements were used to establish an interaction between different areas, such as the pistachio green used in the corridor and bathroom, or the eggplant tones of the living room and bedroom.

The living room's intimate atmosphere
is the result of a combination of straight
lines, some selected pieces of furniture,
and deep, rich colors enhanced by
warm textures such as a thick soft
woolen rug in the sitting room.

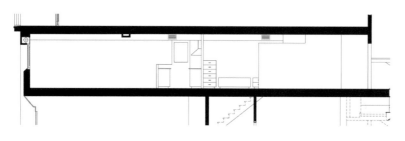

Section

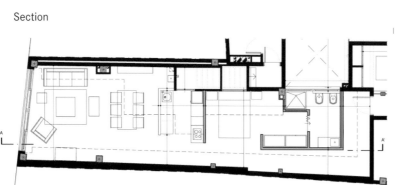

Floor plan

0　1　2

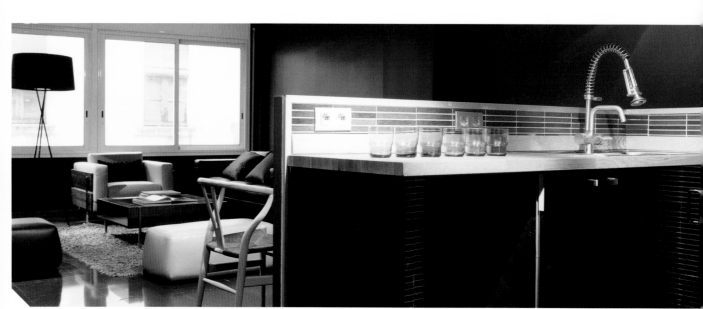

The same lines of coziness and warmth are kept in all the rooms. The bathroom and bedroom are divided by a glass brick wall, which permeates the light and separates functions while preserving intimacy.

Attic in Chueca

Estudio Farini Bresnick

Madrid, Spain, 2004

Despite the lack of space, this small attic was very compartmentalized. Changes centered around the elimination of walls and creation of particular areas. In this way, though the space is continuous, adjustments were made with a limited number of architectural resources: a partition wall, roof windows, a wall of cupboards/shelves, and the bathroom. A partition wall, which serves as an island, separates the bedroom from the living room, providing some privacy while also acting as a headboard. A Velux window in the roof creates an area with zenithlike light. Each room stands out for its different windows; small windows in the bedroom and French windows in the kitchen. Cupboards and shelves extend the entrance wall—the only one at maximum height—creating a storage area with a sliding door to gain space. Finally, the kitchen and bathroom are grouped together to optimize the installations.

The architects made the most of the space, using custom-built cupboards and shelves for clothes, books, and miscellaneous objects. The predominance of white throughout the apartment helps make a fluid space with wooden beams painted in white, wooden MDF carpentry, and the white Macael marble floor. A number of mirrors in the kitchen and bathroom also help enlarge the space.

330 sq ft

Photographs © **Angel Baltanás**

This attic has been designed according to the different heights of the ceiling, placing the bedroom under the lowest height and the kitchen in the opposite corner, where the ceiling is higher.

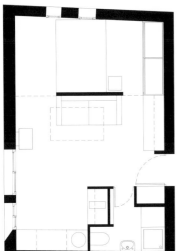

Floor plan

Section

McGrath Loft

Anima Architects

New York, USA, 2003

The segmented floor plan of this apartment in Chelsea neighborhood in Manhattan was transformed into a flexible living and working space. All partitions were removed to create an uninterrupted space and permit natural light to enter. The open area of the apartment accommodates the common spaces, while the bathroom and bedroom were situated in a more isolated area. The walls integrate furniture pieces that optimize the space and emphasize its verticality. Closets were placed behind translucent glass doors. The small, tidy kitchen can be separated from the living room if necessary. The made-to-measure, stainless steel furnishings were designed to conceal the diverse functions. The functional and atmospheric bathroom is characterized by the use of blue stone, mosaic and frosted glass.

590 sq ft

Photographs © **Paúl Rivera/Archphoto**

The extremely small existing bathroom
was remodeled into a condensed box
of blue stone, mosaic and translucent
glass, efficient and atmospheric
at the same time.

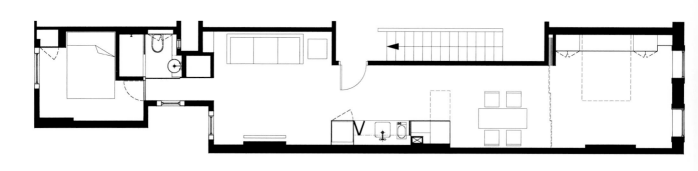

Floor plan

C.E.D.V. House

Filippo Bombace

Rome, Italy, 2003

730 sq ft

Photographs © **Luigi Filetici**

The owners of this residence required a flexible and spacious apartment for hosting frequent parties and informal gatherings. Originally from Naples, the owner chose the colors and materials associated with her background and opted for blue, in representation of the Bay of Naples, as the predominant color for the space. The entry leads into the main space, comprised of the living and dining areas, which is connected to an open kitchen by way of an existing opening between two suspended closets. The kitchen counter and dining table are both made of dark walnut wood. Curtains offer the possibility of isolating either of these areas. The reduced surface area was optimized through the implementation of subtle and simple divisions and the selection of few, yet sizable objects. The entrance also connects with the private areas, which can be closed off with sliding panels. The walls of the bathroom are covered with tiles that feature blue brushstrokes, and the sink rests on a walnut wood counter. Built-in faucets also save on space, and a glass door closes off the shower.

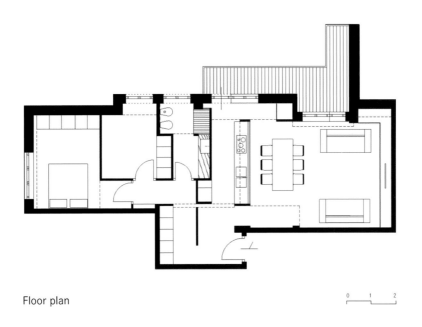

Floor plan

In the bathroom, the glass panel embedded in the wall that isolates the shower provides a depth of view. The functions are separated but the partition is not absolute.

Apartment in Classical Madrid

José Luis Maroto

Madrid, Spain, 2005

This tiny apartment was turned into a cozy home thanks to the remodeling that took into account every last detail in order to make the most of every inch without saturating the space. A wooden module created two main areas, avoiding any drastic separation, which is an essential condition in view of the fact there is only one window for the whole space. Without reducing the brightness, the module was placed in such a way that the light coming from the window reaches both areas. The space is free and fluid with only daily objects on display, thanks to the almost invisible custom-built storage units without handles. The decor is based on very light, folding furniture—which can be put away when not needed—a sofa-bed to put up visitors, and the use of neutral and homogenous colors with little colored brushstrokes to enhance the core of the spaces. The bathroom, located behind the central volume next to the entrance, is separated by a glass partition that allows light to enter. The surfaces were covered with large brown tiles to provide a feeling of intimacy.

380 sq ft

Photographs © **Ángel Baltanás**

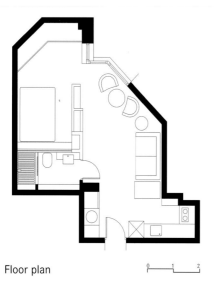

Floor plan

0 1 2

With the exception of the dishwasher, the MDF custom-made furniture in the kitchen was designed with a special depth of twenty inches with polished black slate surfaces.

Apartment in El Born

AAGF Estudio-Grupo CRU

Barcelona, Spain, 2006

In a building in the medieval district of Barcelona, full of stores, trendy restaurants, and a funky atmosphere, one can find this small apartment with a trapezoidal floor plan that, as is typical of many Mediterranean homes, has a small central patio. The renovation consisted of eliminating all the cross brick partitions and substituting them for glass panels, in such a way that the light that enters from the front and the back as well as from the central patio flows freely. A central module was built in laminated birch plywood that is extended along the central hallway. It also includes sliding doors and the storage modules in the kitchen and a nook that has a single bed to accommodate occasional guests or serve as a quiet reading space. The dark wood floor was restored, as well as the brick walls, the arches, and ceiling rafters. To bring out the different textures, light lines were fitted into the sides of the pavement and ceiling, which offer a warm lighting effect. Kitchen and bathroom were both projected with crystal and red MDF cubes. Next to the bathroom, the sleeping area is presided over by a fold-out bed that fits inside a modular structure that runs along the entire apartment. The applied minimalist concept is reinforced and compensated in its historical environment.

710 sq ft

Photographs © **Gogortza & Llorella**

The warmth of the wood and red brick
is highlighted by the use of light, which
creates very cozy atmosphere that is
full of texture.

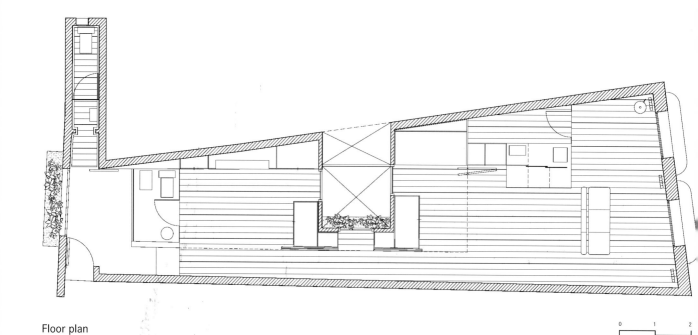

Floor plan

0   1   2

Bathroom and kitchen are encapsulated
in cabins made out of glass and
plywood, combining natural and red
surfaces. The suspended sanitary
elements in the bathroom facilitate the
cleaning and clear up the spaces.

Raper Apartment

Paul Brace Design

Bondi Beach, Australia, 2006

The original structure of this small apartment for a young couple was left intact given the tight budget and the need to seperate the different areas. The smallest room was designated as the bedroom in order to leave as much surface area as possible for daily activities. The apartment was painted entirely in black to disguise its reduced dimensions. The bed was placed on top of a platform that doubles as storage. The largest room was transformed into a dining area, library, and lounge under which objects can be stored away in drawers. The main living space receives the greatest amount of natural light and serves as a meeting, reading, and resting area. Storage solutions have been integrated throughout the apartment, while mirrors were strategically placed to visually multiply the space. A fundamental element of the interior is the illumination created by various spotlights, which were previously used in theater plays, suspended from steel rails along the ceiling, giving the space a scenographic and intimate character. The result is a bold, urban, and highly personalized space.

600 sq ft

Photographs © **Sharrin Rees**

This apartment has two living rooms.
The brightest room has a wide casual
bench with drawers incorporated for
storage. The front living room is
for reading and relaxation.

A mirrored wall in the bathroom helps with the sense of scale in this charcoal tiled cube, while the bedroom is painted black to help conceal the space's small size.

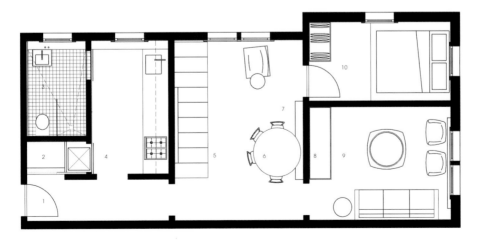

Floor plan

1 Entry

2 Laundry room

3 Bathroom

4 Kitchen

5 Living room

6 Dining room

7 Library

8 Closet

9 Living room

10 Bedroom

0   1   2

Apartment in Sant Feliu

Claudia Schneider, Josep Maria Vivas

Barcelona, Spain, 2005

This residence is located in an apartment complex in Barcelona's metropolitan region. The long distribution hallway can be closed off with sliding doors that separate successive rooms and allow bedrooms to expand and take up the whole breadth of the floor. The height of the walls was closed with glass, so that the perception of space is greater from anywhere in the apartment. Behind the white MDF cupboard in the open entrance hall hides a bathroom. The maroon-tiled bathroom with old hydraulic paving can also be closed with sliding doors. When opened, the bathroom's size extends from the interior wall to the exterior wall. In the bedroom, next to the blue MDF sliding door, a built-in wardrobe with doors in the same material makes a chromatic figure that stands out against the predominant white. In the main room, the stainless steel kitchen is integrated into the living room, and the smoke extractor is wrapped in a white wooden MDF cube. The paving is covered in old hydraulic tiles, which were recovered from another home. Some white MDF shelves were installed between the radiators of the exterior wall to create the same height as the piece of furniture-cum-radiator.

750 sq ft

Photographs © **Eugeni Pons**

A square of the old white brick wall has been left unplastered, as a very simple piece of art that adds texture to the room. The angle next to the window contains a cubical, carved-out fireplace.

The kitchen design is open towards the living room and has been built in stainless steel and glossy MDF, allowing one to appreciate the entire width of this space from this point.

Apartment on Rue St. Fiacre

Philip Harden and Atelier 9 Portes

Paris, France, 2006

540 sq ft

Photographs © **Philippe Harden**

The fundamental objective of this renovation was to revamp an antiquated two-bedroom apartment located in the area of the grand boulevards of Paris. The false ceiling, which had previously been added was removed, gaining nearly over six feet in height that proved very much necessary within such a reduced space. The largest room was converted into the living area with an open kitchen, a single space organized around an island that integrates a kitchen counter. The adjacent dining area enjoys an abundant amount of natural light. An opening was introduced into the central wall of the residence, constituting the backbone of the apartment and housing a bathroom and dressing room that corresponds to the bedroom on the opposite side. The corridor that links the two bedrooms incorporates shelves that run the entire length of the wall. Walls and ceilings were painted white, with the exception of the dark gray central volume that provides some contrasts. The original terra-cotta floors were restored, and its irregular surface produces a vivid, graphic effect.

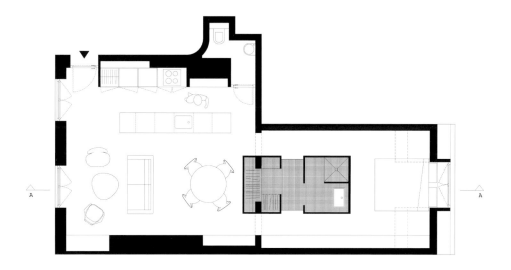

Floor plan

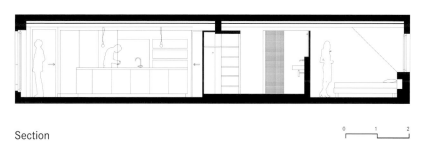

Section

0   1   2

Shelves stretch along the hallway, which connect the two main rooms. Walls and ceilings were painted in white contrasting with the gray color of the central volume and the black tiles in the bathroom.

Joralemon Street Loft

Anima LLC Architecture & Design

Brooklyn, New York, 2005

The architects for this project transformed a dilapidated, two-bedroom residence into a modern and vibrant open-plan apartment by giving it comfort and elegance. The new layout features a sequence of spaces that replaces the traditional compartmentalized scheme, taking advantage of the limited space to integrate various functions at once. In this way, the bedroom serves as a closet, the vestibule can be used as a breakfast room, the living room can be converted into a guest room, and the master bedroom incorporates an office. Closets were built into the walls wherever possible to free up usable space. A reduced palette of colors and materials emphasizes contrasts, which is characterized by the use of bright tones—such as the citric yellow in the kitchen—and by the use of matte versus shine, utilized to create different degrees of transparency that offer visual depth and complement both the na-tural and artificial light.

730 sq ft

Photographs © **Anima LLC Architecture & Design**

The limited floor surface is used efficiently by allowing areas to assume several functions throughout the day. The entrance foyer as breakfast area, the living room as guest room and, the master bedroom as home office.

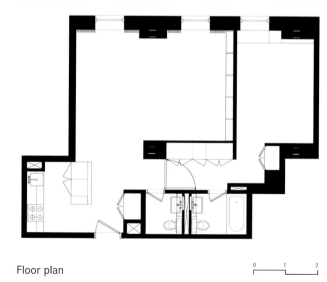

Floor plan

0 1 2

Ronda Loft

**Inés Rodríguez,
Raúl Campderrich/Air Projects**

Barcelona, Spain, 2005

This small and compact attic in the center of Barcelona had a large terrace, which extended the home life to the outdoors in summer. However, the interior space was very fragmented because of its lack of space. Therefore, the kitchen was completely integrated into the living-dining room area, with a worktop, including the faucets and stove, built against the wall and flanked by electrical appliances on the bottom and storage space on the top. White was chosen as the color for all pieces of furniture and allowed the kitchen to blend into the rest of the space. To complete this atmosphere, a solid, simple table receives direct sunlight from the terrace and also serves as a work space for the kitchen. The living room is placed near the terrace, and a small reading area was created in the small space left at the end of the wall.

The private and nighttime spaces are located at the back of the apartment, where a small balcony and two bedroom windows provide access to the exterior. Thanks to the optimum use of space, it was possible to build two bedrooms with two small en suite bathrooms. To standardize the surfaces, the floor was laminated in a gray color, and the bathroom surfaces were covered in black mosaic.

680 sq ft

Photographs © **Jordi Miralles**

Given the limited amount of space, the kitchen is integrated in the living-dining area. The table serves as separation and can be used both as dining place and also as working surface for the kitchen.

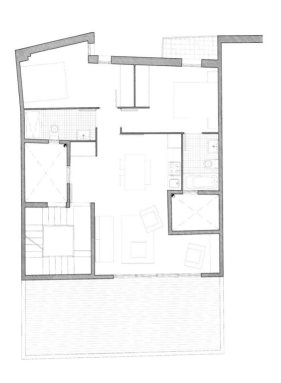

Floor plan

LU.DOmus

Morq Architecture

Rome, Italy, 2004

Located in a classical 1930s building, this apartment was divided into three distinct areas: an open and luminous day area, an intimate night area, and a spacious terrace that adds usable space to the residence.

A continuous closet with shelves and cupboards functions as a partition between the living area and the bedroom, leading to the large terrace. Opposite the entrance, four laminated wood panels can be joined or separated to expose or conceal the shelves and modules. In the bedroom, the same shelving system functions as a wardrobe and generates a warm atmosphere. The bed is elevated onto a platform, leaving space underneath that can be used as storage area.

Abundant light penetrates the windows of the terrace, creating diverse effects as it comes into contact with the different materials. Floors were covered with polished wenge wood, producing a contrast with the brilliant white walls.

700 sq ft

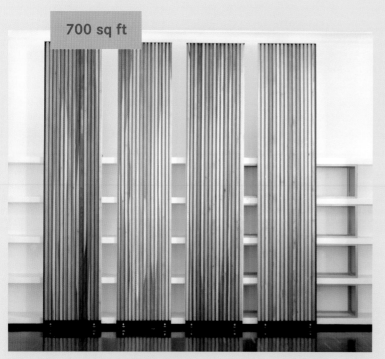

Photographs © **Aliocha Merker**

The built-in bookcases and shelves can
disappear behind sliding Finnish timber
battens, thus transforming the space
into a neat box made clear surfaces.

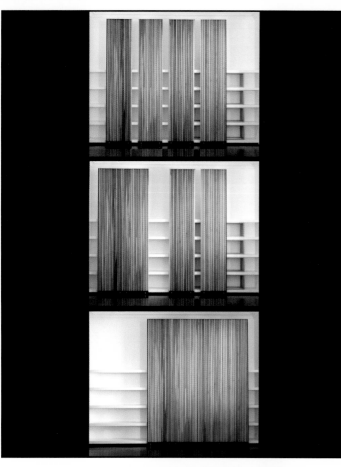

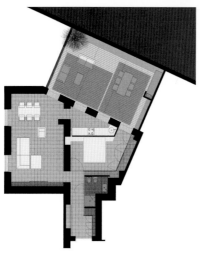

Floor plan

0 1 2

Elements of the original structure of the apartment have prevailed, such as the moldings on walls and ceilings, in contrast with contemporary clean-cut openings without doorframes that give way to the different spaces.

Studio on Thompson Street

Tang Kawasaki Studio

New York, New York, 2005

In designing this small studio in New York's SoHo neighborhood, human scale was greatly taken into account. A series of multifunctional spaces were created to satisfy the needs of the owner. A large part of the common areas were concealed behind a custom-made wooden structure that occupies an entire wall of the apartment and which accommodates a foldout bed, two closets, and storage space for kitchen appliances. The areas can be divided by sliding translucent glass doors. A projection screen placed in front of the facade windows eliminates the need for a place to put the television. The predominating presence of indirect light emitted from within the false ceiling creates subtle forms and volumes, which, together with the use of materials such as dark oak, white concrete, and glass, contribute to the sensation of amplitude.

400 sq ft

Photographs © **Björg Magnea**

The angles between the wall and the
ceiling are illuminated by rows of white
light so that the view is projected
upwards and the height and width of
the room increases.

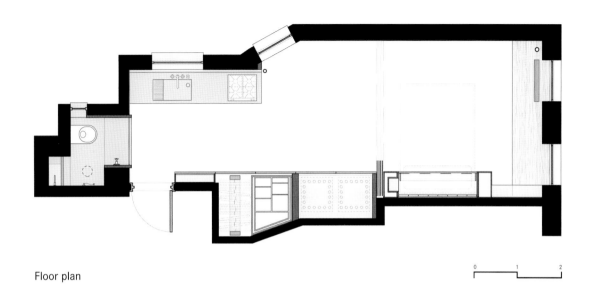

Floor plan

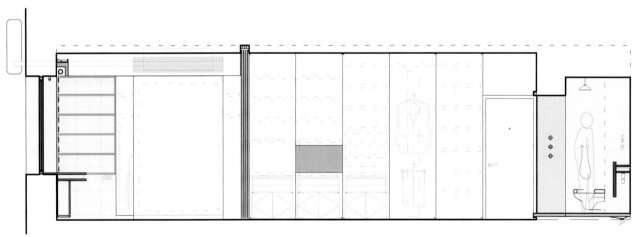

Section

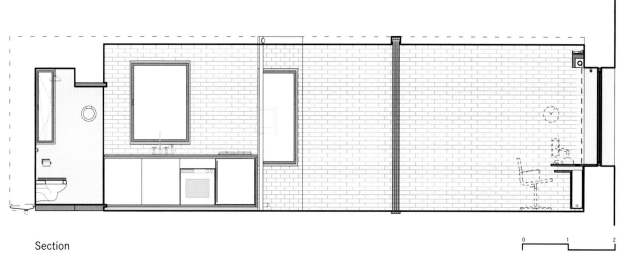

Section

0   1   2

Residence for a Designer

Alberto Marcos & Pablo Sáiz/AMPS

Madrid, Spain, 2004

775 sq ft

Photographs © **Luis Hevia**

This abandoned carpenter's workshop was acquired by a young designer who wanted to transform it into a peaceful refuge in which to live and work, far from the noise and stress of the city center. White was chosen to intensify the atmosphere of tranquility and to lend greater luminosity to the ground floor apartment. An open-plan, fluid space was opted for in order to optimize the entry of light and designated different heights to differentiate the spaces. Next to the galvanized steel and glass door at the entrance, a colorful kitchen enjoys direct daylight. A frosted glass structure encloses the bathroom, which features a platform with the washbasin and a bathtub with a bright orange curtain suspended from a circular rail, which offers a theatrical effect. An air circulation system transforms the bathtub into a cooling system during the summer when filled with cold water. Pivoting MDF panels offer the possibility of closing off the bedroom, located one step up from the bathtub. The space underneath the bed platform can be used as storage area and can be lifted by a pulley system. At the far end of the apartment, a sunken living area makes for a cozy and relaxing space.

The main entrance door is made of steel and etched glass, providing light to work in the kitchen, bringing clarity into the rooms, and allowing necessary intimacy, given the ground floor location of the apartment.

1 Access through entrance hall

2 Bedroom

3 Living room

4 WC

5 Bathroom

6 Kitchen

7 Dining room

8 Yard

9 Studio

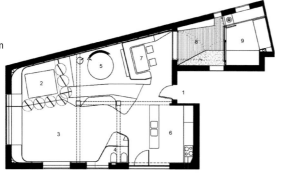

Floor plan

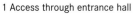

Different functions were set
in individual islands, which revolve
around the central volume containing
the bathtub and the bedroom that is
concealed behind white boards that
pivot on one hinge.

Apartment on Rue Rivoli

Christophe Pillet

Paris, France, 2003

755 sq ft

Photographs © **Vincent Knapp**

This fashion designer's residence and atelier occupies two floors of a Napoleon III-style building located in the center of Paris. The spacious lower floor was designated as the work area and showroom, while the smaller area on the upper floor was used to create the private living quarters. Past and present are combined to generate a luxurious, luminous, and intimate atmosphere. Given the spaciousness of the living room and bedroom, a renovation of the space was not necessary. The unique character of the apartment was emphasized with elegant moldings and coffered ceilings, contrasting off-white tones with the ebony floors. Predominantly white, contemporary furnishings are combined with elaborate, rococo pieces. Large mirrors were strategically placed to heighten the sense of space, and fluffy, white, wool rugs lend texture and comfort to the resting areas.

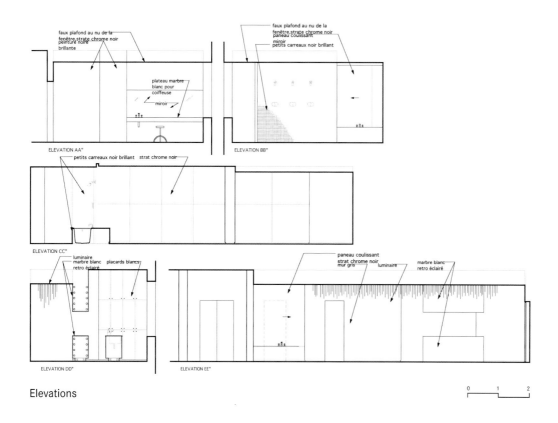

faux plafond au nu de la
fenêtre,strate chrome noir
peinture noire
brillante

plateau marbre
blanc pour
coiffeuse

miroir

ELEVATION AA"

faux plafond au nu de la
fenêtre,strate chrome noir
paneau coulissant
miroir
petits carreaux noir brillant

ELEVATION BB"

petits carreaux noir brillant   strat chrome noir

ELEVATION CC"

luminaire
marbre blanc
retro éclairé
placards blancs

ELEVATION DD"

paneau coulissant
strat chrome noir
mur gris   luminaire

marbre blanc
retro éclairé

ELEVATION EE"

Elevations

0   1   2

Contrasting elements from different styles and periods are framed within a duality of black and white. The thick, soft rug in the living room balances the feeling of spaciousness produced by the generous height of the ceilings.

Apartment in an Industrial Building

Óscar Andreu/AR Interiors

Vilanova i la Geltrú, Spain, 2004

This apartment is located in a previous industrial building, which was reconverted into an apartment block. The architects chose to unify the spaces so that even the bathroom and bedroom would maintain a fluid connection with the remaining areas. In order to define the living room and bedroom, a system of slender, MDF panels painted in bright colors were anchored to the ceiling and floor with steel cables. Drywall partitions conceal the entrance from view and separate the kitchen from the bathroom, raised only partially in order to maintain visual continuity.

The kitchen was given a high-tech and functional appearance, thanks to the linear furnishings, polished surfaces, and stainless steel appliances. A wood kitchen island organizes the space, serves as a bar, and marks the transition into the dining area.

The bathroom, with a dressing area, bathtub, and toilet, was conceived as an extension of the bedroom.

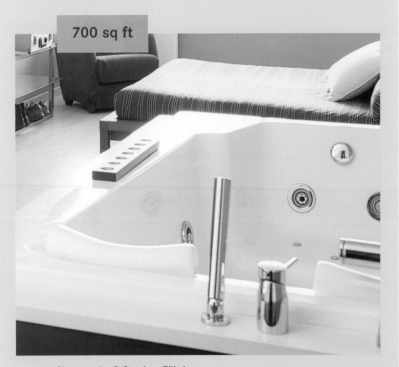

700 sq ft

Photographs © **Stephan Zähring**

The designers boldly removed the partition between the bathroom and the bedroom in order to take advantage of the light. The result is a feeling of spaciousness in both areas, in spite of the restricted amount of space.

Apartment in West Village

AJS Designs

New York, New York, 2006

450 sq ft

Photographs © **Björg Magnea**

The greatest difficulty presented by the renovation of this apartment was to adapt its reduced surface area as both a living and working space for the owner. The bedroom door was relocated at a farther distance from the entrance, providing greater privacy and at the same time granting spaciousness and storage area. The wall that divides the bedroom from the living area and studio integrates closets that can be accessed from either side. A custom-made office table placed in front of the window was designed with the same wood used in the rest of the apartment to lend uniformity to the space. The extended length of the working table also allows it to function as an auxiliary surface for the sofa. An aluminum and translucent glass panel separates the kitchen from the small entrance area, giving character to the entry without creating drastic divisions or preventing the entry of light. The versatility of the components in this residence maximizes a space that was transformed into a practical living and working space despite its reduced surface area and asymmetric configuration.

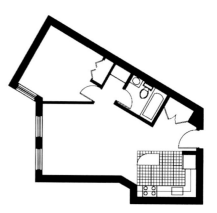

Existing floor plan

New floor plan

0 1 2

Most components in the apartment
serve several functions; for example
the walls between the living area and the
bedroom provide storage on both sides.

Apartment in São Paulo

Fernando Canguçu

Campinas, Brazil, 2005

The interior of this residence is organized on two levels and characterized by the uniformity of the finishings and the flexibility of the layout. The open-plan configuration features interconnected spaces and carefully chosen furnishings. The abundant light that enters through the large windows is further enhanced by the use of white and contrasting details in black, such as the kitchen floor and the wooden furniture. Common spaces around the living room are interconnected. A large polycarbonate panel custom-made by the architect subtly divides the kitchen from the dining area. The wood table in the kitchen, also designed by the architect, functions as an island that separates this area from the adjacent dining room. The living area is organized around a concrete fireplace flanked by large windows. While concrete slabs were chosen for the floors on the lower level, wood was used on the upper level. Austere finishings similarly characterize the luminous bedroom.

730 sq ft

Photographs © **Carlos Emilio**
Jorge Rangel (stylist)

The open kitchen serves as an island, which separates this area from the dining area, which can also be separated by a large polycarbonate movable panel.

Apartment in the West End

Jonathan Clark Studio

London, United Kingdom, 2003

This Victorian building near Regent's Canal was converted during the 1970s into small, fragmented apartments. The renovation eliminated the existing partitions and false ceilings with the aim of creating a more diaphanous space. The result is a large central area that unifies the daily activities, master bedroom, guest room, and bathroom. The cheerful, dynamic, and modern apartment has plenty of storage space and a luminous interior. The kitchen was conceived as a bold and colorful structural element, surrounding by neutral gray tones and polished surfaces. A band of fluorescent light separates the kitchen from the white walls. A large built-in closet between two windows integrates the audiovisual equipment in the living room, which also features indirect lighting techniques that gives a sense of depth to the ceiling. The bathroom surfaces were lined with turquoise mosaic, and the shower is located behind translucent glass panels. A large mirror makes the room seem larger. In the main bedroom, the bed was placed underneath one of the windows, and closets were custom-made.

755 sq ft

Photographs © **Richard Dean**

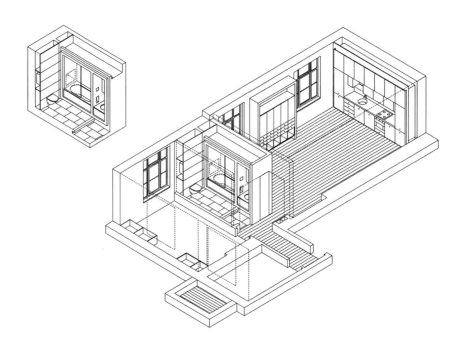

General axonometric and bathroom axonometric

This colorful, contemporary bachelor pad with lots of storage and a feeling of volume and light is result of the opening up of the space and the use of clever lighting.

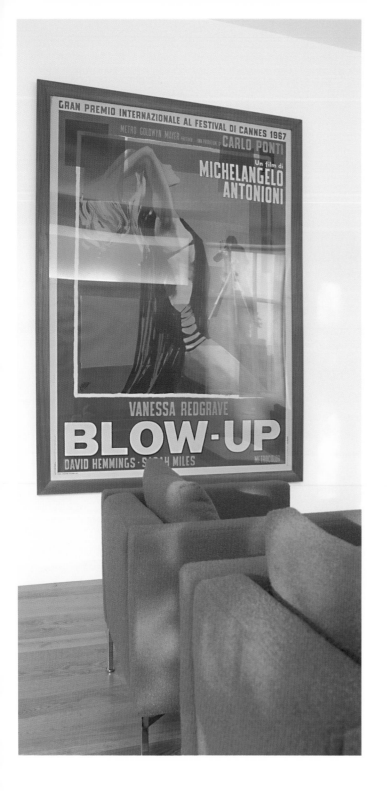

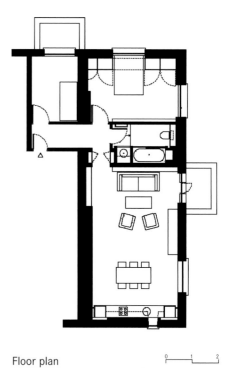

Floor plan

The bathroom on the upper part of this West End apartment is covered in turquoise blue mosaic tiles on one hand, while a large mirror seemingly increases the space. The bed sits between large, yet discreet custom-made wardrobes.

Loft on Las Minas Street

Alejandra Calabrese/Unlugar

Madrid, Spain, 2006

750 sq ft

Photographs © **Luis Hevia**

The designer of this loft located in the center of Madrid is also the owner, and together with her partner, fully renovated this ground floor apartment and semi-basement. Restricted to a low budget, the existing industrial structure was preserved, using bright colors to contrast with the predominating presence of white and concrete. Concrete was used in constructing new elements such as the kitchen and the partitions that divide the space. The main access leads into the living room and kitchen, which is defined by a concrete island that incorporates a sink and also serves as a bar. A wall with two vertical openings isolates the more private areas, including the bedroom, bathroom, and dressing room, all of which feature spotlights and the continued use of concrete. The bedroom is characterized by low-level, dim lighting. The basement—a small area with no exterior access—was transformed into a relaxing reading space that can also double as a guest room. Through the absence of excess partitions and furnishings, the available space of this small apartment is fully optimized.

Industrial construction materials have been preserved, and the designers / owners of this apartment play with lively colors to contrast with the predominant white and cement textures.

The use of cement can be found throughout the apartment. A small room in the basement was turned into a relaxation area, which can easily be transformed into a guest bedroom.

MULTIPLE LEVEL SOLUTIONS

Vandekerkhove-Roelens House

Karien Vandekerkhove

Ghent, Belgium, 2006

720 sq ft

Photographs © **Vercruysse & Dujardin/owi.bz**

In this small house in the historic center of Ghent, a conventional house was divided into small spaces and transformed into a home for contemporary usage where spaces to live and work need to be integrated, with social areas on the one side and private ones on the other.

Despite being located on a narrow street, the house has enough windows to inundate all corners with natural light. However, to make the most of a scarce resource in this North Atlantic region, a large skylight was built into the slanting roof, which helps to illuminate the house's central area, where the staircase is located. The main room is the kitchen, which shares a space with the dining area and home office. A large piece of furniture with plenty of drawers hides and stores all office supplies. The piece of furniture is painted in black to coordinate with the room's walls, and the drawers are marked with white letters. Thus, through a chromatic uniformity, the wall turns into a kitchen blackboard, and the kitchen table can, on occasion, even turn into a work space. A small breakfast area was installed in the passage between the kitchen and bathroom. The master bedroom, bathroom, and storage room are located on the second floor, where most of the books are kept. A mezzanine was built in order to house a library, which extends to the roof.

The huge custom-made wooden filing cabinet was painted in black so that it fuses with the wall behind. Its capability allows the remaining space to be always tidy and clean.

House HP

Architecton, Masahiro Ikeda

Meguro, Japan, 2004

660 sq ft

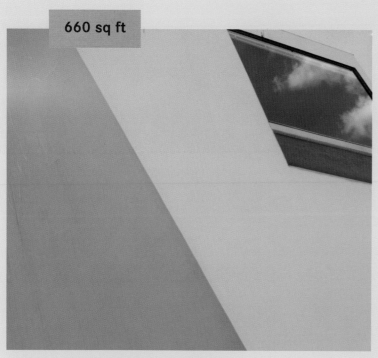

Photographs © **Roberto Giostra/owi.bz**

This vertiginous house is raised in the middle of a series of very narrow backstreets. To make the most of the available land, the architects raised a wooden structure that twists around itself. In a dramatic gesture, the hyperbolic-parabolic (HP) surface works on a sculptural, functional, and structural flat space, making room for a parking space adjacent to the street, and a light-absorbing panel, which spreads light throughout all levels of the house. The bathroom, wardrobe, and small entrance hall can be found on the ground floor. A flight of stairs climbs parallel with the inclined wall to the second floor where the kitchen-living room area is located. A railing with a mesh structure surrounds the hole of the staircase on this floor and does not obstruct the view. The space set aside for meetings is located just beneath a red cube, which, in fact, contains the bedroom on the third floor. In between these two levels, an almost invisible spiral staircase seems to lead to the sky, thanks to the see-through glass cover that allows light to enter. The bedroom is made of wood and painted in a bright red color. The bed was placed on a platform, which incorporates the storage space and is elevated up to the window, allowing a view of the outdoor vegetation. A small ladder leads to the solarium.

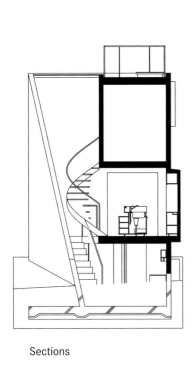

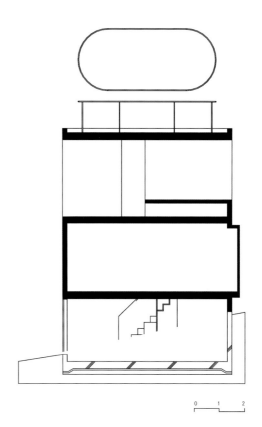

Sections

0　1　2

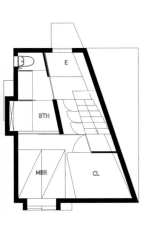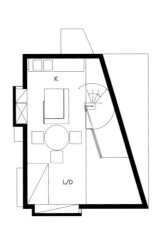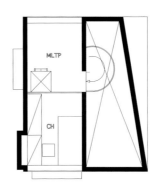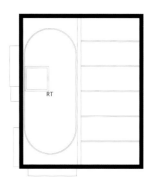

Floor plans

0　1　2

Half of the roof was opened with
a skylight that illuminates the inside
of the building from above so that
the light reflects upon the convex
surfaces of the walls.

Mini Loft in Rome

Morq Architecture

Rome, Italy, 2005

645 sq ft

Photographs © **Aliocha Merker**

The starting point for this project was a rectangular floor plan and a sloping wood ceiling with a height of over 16 feet. Three windows on the main facade provide abundant natural light. The owner wanted to divide the apartment into three floors, placing the day areas on the lower level. In order to create a space for the dressing room, a structure was created that became the central architectural feature of the project: a lightweight steel and PVC unit as tall as the mezzanine, which holds the staircase and a small storage area in addition to the dressing room. The bedroom occupies the entire mezzanine. The red PVC volume adds a colorful note to the neutral space, while the perforated steel staircase filters views from the entrance through to the main space. When the screen is moved, the staircase is concealed from view. The kitchen is organized around a concrete island that integrates the kitchen appliances and cupboards. "Poor" materials were chosen in response to a limited budget and the desire to employ a simple design.

Running parallel to the kitchen counter, the red PVC volume, the only chromatic element of the project, hides a dressing and storage unit and gives the impression of supporting the mezzanine.

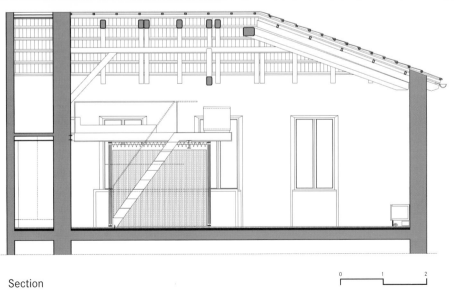

Section

0   1   2

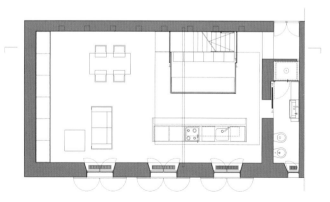

Ground floor

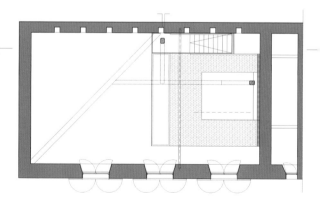

Mezzanine

Mezzanine on Top of a Wardrobe

Beriot Bernardini

Madrid, Spain, 2005

The advantage of this apartment is the eleven-foot-high ceiling, which compensated for the limited space. Creating a mezzanine was the only way of gaining space, which gave this home an extra 91 square feet on the second floor. The structure was exclusively designed in MDF and separates four different spaces of different heights—two upstairs and two downstairs.

The lower part of the structure houses the closet, made of an extractable cupboard with two wheels that come from under the staircase. The seven-foot-deep wardrobe consists of two modules on wheels that can be organized according to season, as one can be more accessible than the other, thanks to the sliding stairs. Another cupboard in the adjoining space hides the refrigerator, and a seven-foot-tall walk-in closet was built above the storage modules, while the kitchen can be hidden away by a panel of folding doors. The bathroom is located opposite the wardrobes by the entrance. The bedroom is located on top of the kitchen and measures five feet in height, enough to sit down or lie down. An industrial platform of solid oak is used for the flooring. Indirect light from the ceiling creates a soft atmosphere, and the furniture is made of the same white lacquered wood as the mezzanine structure.

381 sq ft

Photographs © **Ángel Baltanás**

To make the most of this small apartment with very high ceilings, the space was divided into different areas of varying heights. The lower space contains a wardrobe, which rolls out from underneath the stairs.

Apartment in Brasilia

Fernandes & Capanema

Brasilia, Brazil, 2006

720 sq ft

Photographs © **Fernandes & Capanema**

This project was commissioned by a journalist who wanted to live in an apartment with a minimum of obstacles, furniture, and color. The predominant use of white and silver offsets the apartment's low height on the second floor. It was also necessary to obtain a calm and serene atmosphere, a refuge from the owner's hectic life. The designers aimed for a total fluidity of space in an apartment that had previously been covered in dark wood, with various compartments and a huge staircase—out of proportion with the home's small size. The kitchen-dining room and a small bathroom can be found on the ground floor; this is the only area that was isolated by a silver-plated glass panel. The resident also requested an integrated space where he could attend to his guests while cooking. The old staircase had to be replaced with a new, less obtrusive one, in order to fit the dining room table. Kitchen cupboards were replaced with a cupboard with a sliding sliver-plated glass panel. When closed, this panel forms the backdrop for the work area and when open it is a common area and pantry. An intimate area with a bed, changing room, desk, and bathroom was created on the top floor. The glass divisions and mirrors separate the areas without creating any drastic divisions. The warm illumination based on yellow tones contrasts with the neutral effect of the predominant cold colors throughout the apartment.

The ethereal, spiral staircase seems to be suspended in the air and connects the daytime areas to the private rooms on the upper floor.

Lofts in Glorieta de Quevedo

Manuel Serrano Arquitectos

Madrid, Spain, 2006

The renovation of this building in the old part of Madrid transformed an old factory into four individual residences. Originally 530 square feet each, 210 square feet were added to each apartment thanks to the addition of mezzanines made possible by the generous height of the ceilings. Based on the typical 1970s lofts of New York, the transformation called for an open-floor plan, a pronounced industrial character, and the combination of living and working spaces. The central pillar of the structure was turned into spiral staircase that leads to a mezzanine housing the bathroom and a possible bedroom. One of the particularities of these residences is the presence of prefabricated materials, with the exception of concrete used for the beams and the stair wall. The steel and glass staircase evokes images of French engineers and Russian constructivism. The steps are finished in painted plaster. Parquet floors provide a sophisticated look, and brick walls were varnished. All metallic elements were restored and varnished, while the metallic pieces of the interior were painted with Oxyron Martelé.

740 sq ft

Photographs © **Manuel Serrano Arquitectos**

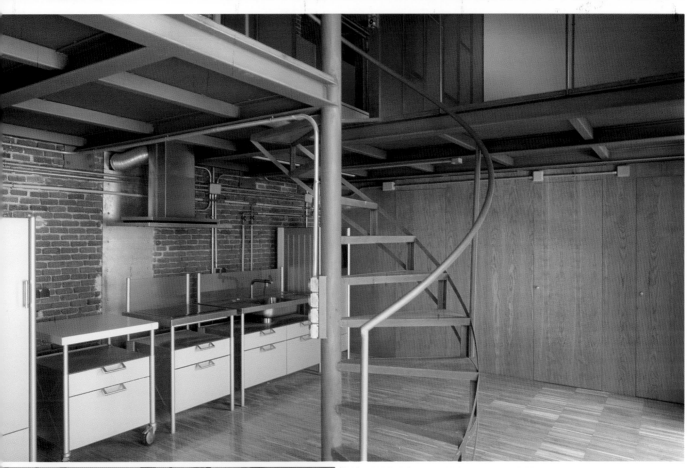

The glass-and-steel staircase allows natural clarity to penetrate the apartment from the skylight on the roof. The visible pipes and services and the old brick wall emphasize the industrial aspects of these apartments.

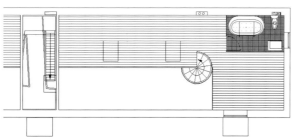

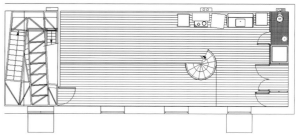

Mezzanine

Ground floor

0 1 2

Apartment for a Musician

Lola Lago Interiores

Rubí, Spain, 2004

750 sq ft

Photographs © **Eugeni Pons**

This previously commercial space was transformed by the designer Lola Lago to serve two purposes: a studio and residence for her musician son and a showroom that showcases the transformation of a small space. The space consisted of a small 430-square-foot rectangle distributed over three levels and a small mezzanine with a bathroom. The different ceiling heights of the ground floor were maintained, designating the lowest space as the bedroom. The small corridor, scarcely six feet in height, was converted into a guest room with the addition of sofa bed. The bedroom ceiling integrates a skylight that can be uncovered to allow light to filter through from the upper level. A wardrobe next to the bedroom is separated from the studio by a curtain. The level underneath incorporates the entrance and bathroom, and the staircase was placed along the facade in order not to block the entry of light. The existing bathroom on the upper floor was conserved, and the structural wall was replaced with a glass panel. In addition to the living and working areas, a multifunctional space was created to serve as a meeting or dining area. Many furnishings and materials from the original offices were integrated into the new design, and existing elements such as the ceramic floors were preserved in this small and low-budget project.

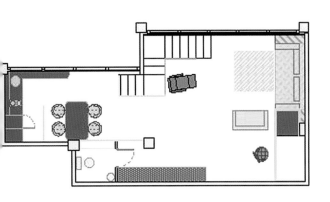

Ground floor

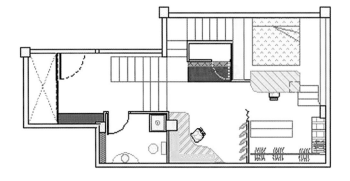

Mezzanine

0 1 2

This apartment's imaginative design reflects the needs of its owner. It manages to fit out a space for every function, including those designed for recording and informal work meetings.

Vila Grandela

FFCB Arquitectos Associados

Lisbon, Portugal, 2006

Although the reduced dimensions of this tiny apartment made it seem practically impossible to create a fully equipped, contemporary residence, the challenge resulted in a magical transformation of the space. Located in the working-class residential complex of Barrio Grandela, constructed at the beginning of the twentieth century, the apartment had never undergone renovation and thus had to be completely redesigned. The upper floor was conceived as a mezzanine, allowing it to be seen from the lower floor. Spaces were redistributed and functions were combined in order to eliminate superfluous elements. The layout revolves around a central volume that integrates the sanitary installations and vertical access to the upper floor, enabling circulation and visual contact between the different spaces. The small mezzanine accommodates the bedroom and storage area, while the lower floor houses the day area and the bathroom. Existing structural elements were left exposed in honor of the original space and the date of its construction.

390 sq ft

Photographs © **Fernando Guerra**

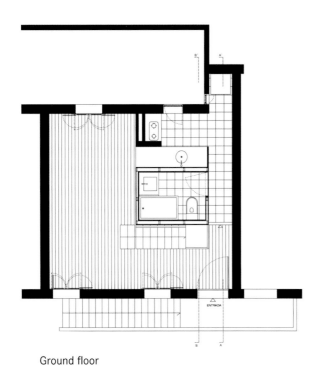

Ground floor

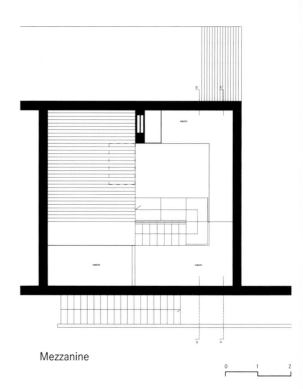

Mezzanine

0   1   2

The spaces were brought together, and functions were redistributed. Some elements have preserved the essence of the past in a unique fusion of textures.

Studio on Escorial Street

Javier Hernández Mingo

Madrid, Spain, 2004

750 sq ft

Photographs© **Luis Hevia**

This old warehouse was completely renovated in order to create a home that could also be a work place. Though this floor went through a serious transformation, certain elements referring to the space's industrial past were preserved, such as the structural beams that were exposed. The architects wanted uniformity in the basic elements in order to make different areas and atmospheres stand out, using warm-colored pieces of furniture. The floor was leveled with polished cement, and straight lines, both vertical and horizontal, such as pillars, beams and stairs, were added throughout the apartment. In contrast, the dining area has plenty of curves, both in the furniture and the decorative elements. The bathroom, an open area facing the dining room, was built on a white-streaked marble platform and can be reached by two steps from the living room, thus creating a small informal meeting area. It is closed by a combination of different white curtains. Making the most of the place's height, a mezzanine was built for the bedroom, underneath which kitchen utensils and a large closet are located.

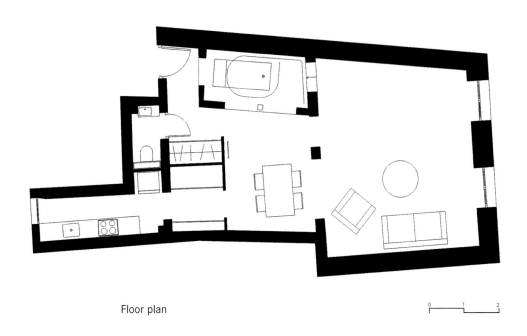

Floor plan

0   1   2

The bathtub, with its streaked white marble surfaces and theatrical curtains, is the only luxurious element among the otherwise humble selection of materials that represent the industrial past of the apartment.

Apartment in Buenos Aires

Miguel Bornstein

Buenos Aires, Argentina, 2003

The antiquarian Miguel Bornstein acquired this apartment in a classical building in northern Buenos Aires as a place in which to display all the objects that he had accumulated throughout his travels. Despite the quantity of objects and diversity of styles, the interior design achieves a perfect balance of eclecticism and clarity, partially thanks to the square and diaphanous floor plan. The various levels contribute fluidity and organize the different volumes. The apartment has access to the exterior on both sides. A large glass window from floor to ceiling opens up to the courtyard allowing daylight to penetrate throughout. The built-in shelves also aid in creating an uncluttered environment, providing a place for books and decorative objects. Photographs, contemporary artworks, a valuable library, and numerous collection items, such as old toys made by the owner, all give a fascinating atmosphere to this luminous apartment.

740 sq ft

Photographs © **Virginia del Giudice**

The generous amount of light and the neat structure of the apartment have made it possible to organize a small space within a classical structure, in such a way that all the beloved objects can be included without losing the feeling of spaciousness.

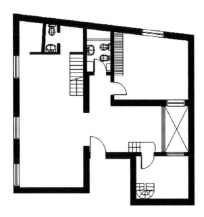

Floor plan

0 1 2

House in the Center of Ghent

Raymond Jacquemyns

Ghent, Belgium, 2005

740 sq feet

Photographs © **Bart van Leuven**

The designer Raymond Jacquemyns transformed this old and narrow house in the city's old town for a friend, turning it into a space that reflected the owner's spirit. Rectangular windows were opened in the facade to allow as much light as possible to enter from the narrow street. Inside, the structures were simplified, leaving cement on view, while the floor was treated and varnished, maintaining its aged color.

A simple kitchen was built on the ground floor, using pure lines that combine the use of dark oakwood with clear and warm cement. On the other side of the small hallway, the dining room was placed in an open space and contains an old wooden plank and a rectangular table as mirror surface, its sheen contrasting with the relative coarseness of the predominant materials. Small holes were made in the ceiling above the table, and small yellow lights were inserted. A modernist spiral staircase with a carved wooden handrail leads to the second floor, where gray cement predominates. Adjacent to the living room with built-in chimney, is a small breakfast or meeting area. A red velvet chaise lounge is a contrast to the general austerity. A light, projecting staircase leads to the top floor where the bedroom, bathroom, and wardrobe space can be found.

Several details speak of the art deco past of the building, such as the wooden spiral staircase or the cast-iron fireplace that presides the living room on the first floor.

The interiors combine classical elements with more radical additions, such as the cantilevered staircase that leads to the upper floor or the use of concrete in walls and ceilings.

Darlinghurst Apartment

Greg Natale Interior Design

Sydney, Australia, 2005

This small apartment in the center of Sydney is a small gem. The owner and designer, Greg Natale, wanted a design that would reflect his passions and cultural identity, including his Italian background, the vibrant 1970s in which he grew up, and the contemporary environment in which he has evolved. His Italian roots are expressed through elements typical of Italian homes, such as bold basalt surfaces, a Murano lamp, and an ebony sideboard. Certain furnishings, such as the coffee table and dining chairs evoke a 1970s style, as does the use of mirrors, which also serves to magnify the space. The dark gray walls, which challenge the small dimensions of the space, were compensated by the sparsity of furnishings and the large windows that lead to the terrace to provide abundant daylight. A significant gain in surface area was generated by the unification of the entrance hall, dining room, and kitchen, behind which the living room is located. Here, the sofa is placed against a wall that conceals the staircase leading to the mezzanine where the bedroom and bathroom are housed. A simple organization creates a warm and sensual atmosphere.

730 sq ft

Photographs © **Sharrin Rees**

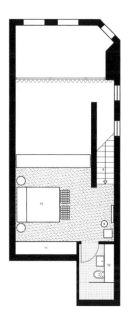

Ground floor   Mezzanine

To create drama and a contrast from the rest of the white building, this apartment was painted in charcoal gray. A honed basalt floor and a fur rug add richness and glamour to this space.

Taffeta curtains and 1970s design elements add a theatrical element to the dining and living areas. The open plan's kitchen features mirrors, turning it into a wet bar.

Duplex in Malasaña

Rocío Fueyo Casado

Madrid, Spain, 2005

600 sq ft

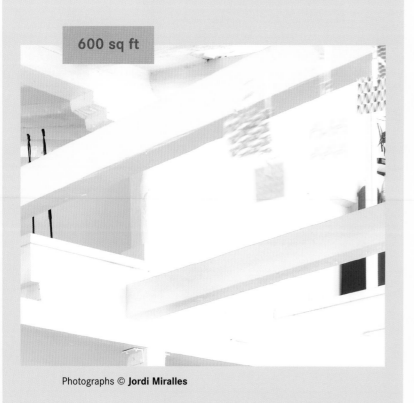

Photographs © **Jordi Miralles**

The renovation of this interior in a typical residential building of Madrid was carried out with very few resources. The neglected living space was first undertaken by the owner, who later commissioned the project to a construction company. The furniture were primarily found at flea markets and closing down offices. All internal walls were removed, exposing the wooden beams underneath the attic and enabling the aperture of eight windows that significantly increased the entry of natural light. The elimination of the false ceiling granted a new height of sixteen feet, which permitted the construction of a 172-square-foot mezzanine designated as bedroom and small guest room. A cantilevered staircase inspired by Jacques Tati's film *Mon Oncle* was erected in the center of the space, along with another one fixed to the wall reminiscent of the emergency staircases employed by subway operators. Preferring a larger living area, the owner opted for a small yet functional kitchen and bathroom. Light parquet was chosen for the floor of the living areas, while tiles were used for the kitchen. All surfaces were painted white, with the exception of one structural wall, which was painted bright orange, a color echoed by various elements to create a cheerful and luminous atmosphere.

The walls and ceiling of this apartment were torn down, changing its distribution completely. Windows were opened letting the sun shine in for 6 hours a day.

Ground floor

Mezzanine

0   1   2

Apartment in Attic

Geneviève Marginet

Brussels, Belgium, 2003

This small attic was remodeled as a temporary residence while the rest of the house underwent a longer and more expensive renovation. Being a temporary home, the owners—a designer and interior designer—decided to experiment boldly with new formulas and elements to simplify life in such a small space. They took their inspiration from design and futuristic films from 1960s and 1970s. Both the walls and the furniture have rounded organic shapes, which are very appropriate for small spaces. Curved holes were cut in the walls as built-in shelves. A long piece of furniture was built to merge the space and group the various activities. The kitchen's work surface is extended to the sink and kitchen furniture. A useful wall was built around this chain leading from the kitchen to the bathroom and makes up the kitchen furniture, oven, bathroom storage (which is reached through a door inspired by spaceships), the bathroom sink, and shower. As these pieces were designed and made by the owners, it was possible to transform and adapt them as necessary. The bedroom is located above the capsule, which encloses the bathroom. The brown strip, which decorates the area around the kitchen sink, is elevated to this height, where its thickness increases and converts into a work space.

410 sq ft

Photographs © **Vercruysse & Dujardin/owi.bz**

Inspired by 1960s and 70s futuristic films, this small attic's walls and furniture have rounded, organic shapes. All kitchen elements are merged into one custom-built piece of furniture.

The bathroom capsule is located underneath the bedroom. Cut-out holes serve as shelving throughout the apartment and can be customized to fit other elements such as the bathroom mirror.

Duplex in Greenwich Village

Peter Tow/Tow Studios

New York, New York, 2005

In renovating this small duplex located in the heart of Manhattan, a staircase was designed to connect the daytime areas on the lower level with the nighttime areas on the upper level. The existing layout gave way to a unique space with the character of a loft. Despite a reduced budget and thanks to the double-height ceilings, a bedroom and two bathrooms were created on the upper floor. A minimalist kitchen features integrated appliances underneath a countertop that extends lengthwise to provide as much working space as possible. A wooden board separates the kitchen and living room and creates an informal dining area that can also be used as a bar or breakfast area. The upper floor overlooks the living room and offers panoramic views of the city.

700 sq ft

Photographs © **Björg Magnea**

The double height living area of this one-bedroom duplex in Greenwich Village is overlooked by the main bathroom. A frosted glass wall separates the two spaces.

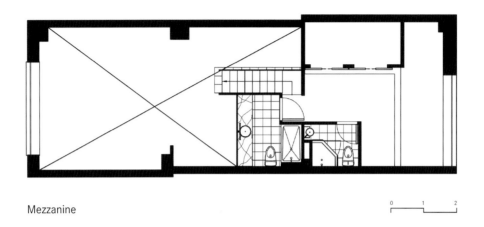

Mezzanine

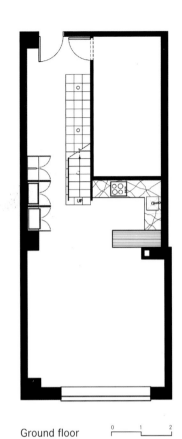

Ground floor

0 1 2

The bedroom and bathroom upstairs are connected to the living room and kitchen downstairs by a new staircase, designed to feel "light" and "open."

Little Fisherman's House

Peter Ivens/Astra

Knokke, Belgium, 2005

700 sq ft

Photographs © **Verne/owi.bz**

This small fishing house in the center of the coastal town of Knokke was purchased with the intention of maintaining its structure and timeless atmosphere. Behind an extremely narrow facade hides a spacious home, in spite of its small size. The entrance leads into the ground floor's only space, where all partitions have been removed to create a living room and a kitchen. The kitchen sink and dishwasher are located behind the staircase, which leads to the two top floors. The remaining kitchen elements can be found in the great central block, which takes up a large part of the room. The block creates an island that incorporates the stovetop and oven on one side and creates a large and comfortable table on the other. This practical and informal style brings together two functions, allowing people to enjoy the whole space while cooking. The old chimney, located opposite the staircase and part of the whitewashed brick wall, helps to create a warm atmosphere in the dining area. A closed terrace on this floor is used as a dining room and relaxation area when the weather is nice. The only bedroom on the first floor is in a small and cozy living area, which is easily turned into an improvised guest room. The main bedroom, with en suite bathroom, on the top floor makes the most of the height. A wardrobe made of terraced modules leads to another wardrobe placed higher up.

The wet kitchen facilities were fitted under the staircase, making room for the cooking surface in the middle of the room where one can work and enjoy company at the same time.

Studio on Madison Avenue

Kar-Hwa Ho

New York, USA, 2006

Situated on the fifteenth floor of a 1940s building, this small studio had a long and narrow floor plan with a bathroom and kitchen that had no access to the exterior. The challenge was to make the most of the high ceilings and transform the space into an oasis of calm and simplicity by bringing in light and views. Another objective was to open up as much storage space as possible and better integrate the kitchen and bathroom for a more fluid configuration. A trail of lights illuminate the narrow entrance area, leading to the main living space, in which the bedroom is defined by a platform that supports the bed and doubles as a wardrobe and storage unit. Illuminated from behind, a wooden bench seemingly floats along the length of the space and serves as a shelf. A translucent glass panel separates the bedroom from the kitchen, allowing light to penetrate the kitchen while keeping it out of sight. Mosaic and marble were used for the bathroom surfaces. The new quality of light maximizes the feeling of spaciousness in these areas as well as in the rest of the apartment.

590 sq ft

Photographs © **Björg Magnea**

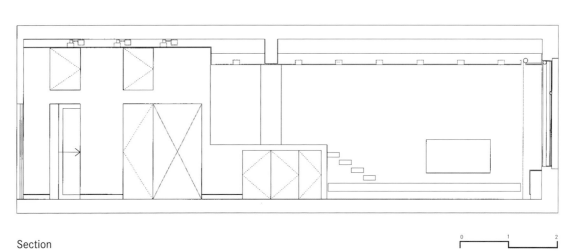

Section

0　　　1　　　2

The kitchen and bathroom of this fifteenth-floor Manhattan apartment are windowless rooms. A sandblasted glass wall in the kitchen and a frosted glass window in the bathroom allow natural light to enter.

SMART
SOLUTIONS

Carlton Ramsey Apartment

Paul Brace Design

Sydney, Australia, 2005

Situated on the twenty-second floor of an iconic building in the center of Sydney, this one-bedroom apartment is used as a residence during the week by a journalist couple who lives on the coast. Despite its reduced size, the apartment offers spectacular views over the city, which visually enhance the sense of amplitude. Without making any changes to the structure, the living room was rearranged to define the different areas with more clarity. The larger furniture pieces were placed against the walls to free up space, making room for noble materials and luxurious fabrics that provide warmth and intimacy. A bench upholstered in black leather was placed parallel to the wall, orientating the view towards the balcony and defining the living room opposite the dining room. Contrasting materials such as oak and black lacquer were used to generate the sensation of comfort and repose desired by the tenants. The corridor wall was lined with the same wood to create a sense of continuity, while mirrors were placed in the entrance hall to offset its reduced dimensions.

700 sq ft

Photograhs © **Sharrin Rees**

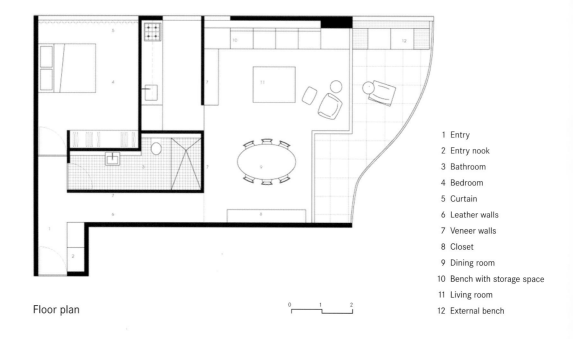

Floor plan

0 1 2

1 Entry
2 Entry nook
3 Bathroom
4 Bedroom
5 Curtain
6 Leather walls
7 Veneer walls
8 Closet
9 Dining room
10 Bench with storage space
11 Living room
12 External bench

The living room, open towards the city skyline, and the bedroom's intimate atmosphere correspond to the residents' needs, who required a lively entertaining area and a peaceful pad for relaxing.

Perraton Apartment

Stephen Varady Architecture

Sydney, Australia, 2003

430 sq ft

Photographs © **Stephen Varady**

The design of this apartment aims to give functionality and fluidity to the space and create practical areas that enhance the illusion of space through the exploration of volumes. The project develops around the creation of volumetric forms without sacrificing practical aspects. The interior spaces function as a series of rectangular prisms derived from straight lines that clearly define the space, employing concepts such as the arkhitektons by Kazimir Malevich. The intersection of these prisms allows for the exploration of volumetric possibilities when associated with practical applications. The kitchen is comprised of intersecting elements that can be folded, slid, or opened to reveal the contents. Similarly, the bathroom and bedroom doors were substituted with sliding panels, and the dining table can be folded away. The television is suspended in a box from the ceiling that conceals the cables and rotates so that it can be viewed from anywhere inside the apartment. A large mirror opposite the windows reflects the spectacular views of the bay that could otherwise only be obtained from a small corner. The mobility of the pieces that comprise this residence allow for a flexible atmosphere that adapts to the changing needs of the resident.

The kitchen disappears when the table is lifted, so that the living room doubles its space. The custom-made modules have no handles and, thanks to their different, volumes become an imaginative piece of art.

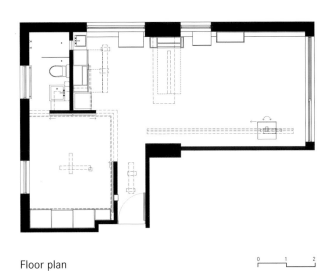

Floor plan

Small Industrial Apartment

Nicolas Vignot

Paris, France, 2002

This small loft is located on the first floor of a building in Paris that dates back to 1850 when it was used as a stable. It was later converted into a metal workshop and recently transformed into a residential block. The small, rectangular space had no partitions and windows along one wall. The two main objectives of the project were to optimize the entry of natural light and provide different perspectives through the use of mobile partitions. The apartment was divided into two areas: a large and diaphanous space and another space that incorporated plastic and glass divisory panels similar to Japanese shoji screens but with an industrial look. The common areas were left exposed to reinforce this concept. During the day, the panels can be opened or closed to create different environments. The walls that separate the bedroom from the bathroom and kitchen are incomplete, allowing natural light to reach all corners of the apartment. Between the bedroom and kitchen, the wall is simply comprised of brick and glass panels, letting in light while isolating the private area from the common areas. The architect designed the furniture in the living area, and a warm atmosphere is created thanks to the fireplace in one corner.

515 sq ft

Photographs © **Paolo Bevilacqua**

Foor plan

0 1 2

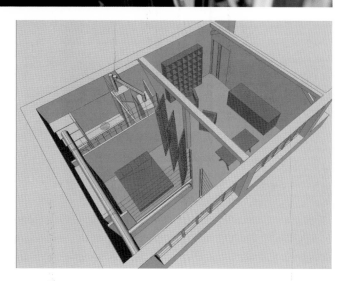

Perspective

The use of red color in walls and fabrics creates a certain intimate atmosphere in the bedroom, in a dwelling where all the partitions are transparent and removable, and the different atmospheres can be fused into each other.

Player's Pad

Rafael Berkowitz

New York, USA, 2006

742 sq ft

Photographs © **James Wilkins**

In designing this apartment, the architect was inspired by the extravagant production design of the film *American Psycho*. The central piece of the space is a dining room with a double ceiling lit from within, emitting a band of light that runs along the entire length of the wall and creates different atmospheres. Adjacent to the living area, the integrated kitchen is comprised of stainless steel furnishings combined with black wood cupboards and acid-etched glass doors. The living room was situated opposite the dining area in order to take advantage of the spectacular views of the city. Sliding doors were made with white lacquered wood and opalescent glass panels. The luxurious and sophisticated interior also provides a great deal of comfort. In the master bedroom, a custom-made canopy bed placed on top of a platform incorporates spotlights that reflect light off the ceiling, creating a cavelike effect and a comforting dim atmosphere. The use of noble materials unifies the different spaces while also providing the necessary contrast.

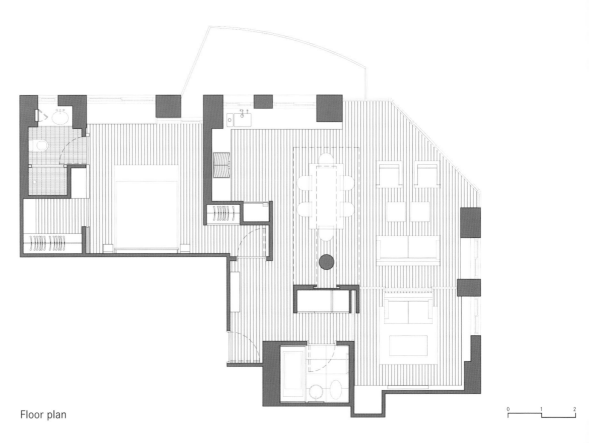

Floor plan

0   1   2

Glass etched panels divide the
little studio from the living area.
When closed, they still allow light
to filter through.

U-shaped island wall was raised between the little hall, the dining and living rooms and the studio, so that it houses a deep wardrobe and organizes the adjacent spaces.

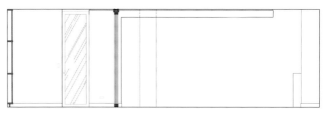

Den/living room section

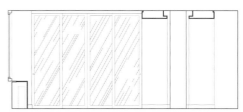

Living/dining room section

0 1 2

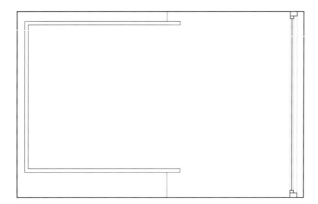

Bed/canopy side section

Bayswater Apartment

Andy MacDonald/Mac Interactive

Sydney, Australia, 2003

745 sq ft

Photographs © **Tom Ferguson**

The rectangular layout of the main space in this apartment contains a terrace that lends an advantageous L-shaped floor plan and an abundant amount of daylight. The space was conceived as shared living space in which cooking and dining were a priority. The owners desired a functional and spacious kitchen that could be easily concealed when not in use. In order to achieve this goal, the same materials were chosen for the kitchen and living room to create uniformity. Instead of placing storage modules underneath the sink and stove, the kitchen furniture incorporates discreet cupboards and drawers. Taps can also be concealed behind the wall when not in use. A dining table placed parallel to the walls is perceived as a continuous surface that culminates in the red Perspex panels. The living room was conceptualized as an extension of the entrance and corridor that joins with the terrace. The corridor provides access to the bedrooms, a bathroom, and a studio that doubles as a guest room.

Large windows, which are kept open all
year round thanks to the area's mild
climate, allows the terrace to become
part of the living room.

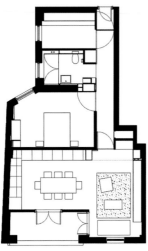

Floor plan

0 1 2

The master bedroom in this city apartment enjoys plenty of natural light thanks to the adjacent terrace.

The studio can easily be transformed into a guest bedroom by folding away part of the work space.

Interior Cabins

Marc Amyot

Montreuil, France, 2004

730 sq ft

Photographs © **Pierrick Bourgoin**

This old Letraset factory was entirely gutted out, removing all interior partitions to make room for a spacious residence. The owners, an artist and an actor with a passion for the outdoors, gave the space a rustic character by adding two cabins that function as the bedroom and bathroom. The remaining floor plan was left open and holds the common areas. The wood cabins open out to the exterior through windows that were integrated into the walls. Wood scraps, which were polished and restored, were used to make the wooden planks that line the floors, while the wood used for the cabins was recycled from an old wood manufacturer. The kitchen is located in front of the cabin that houses the bathroom, and the window that joins them is used to hang kitchen utensils. A display cabinet provides a subtle transition into the main space. Objects and furniture found on the street and bought at flea markets and antique shops decorate the interior and create intimate areas such as the working desk, living room, and dining room. Only one of the shelf units occupies the entire height of the space, generating a clean and uncluttered environment.

The two cabins function as separate
atmospheres inside the apartment:
according to each moment,
they allow different degrees
of intimacy.

Apartment on the Atlantic Coast

Huiswerk Architecten

Zeebrugge, Belgium, 2003

This small summer apartment is located on the Belgian coast, close to Bruges. It could be summed up as a cupboard and a table, as the cupboard turns into the bedroom, and the table becomes the kitchen. Thanks to clever carpentry, all activities are integrated in a few organic and clean-cut pieces, leaving the space clear—a commendable quality in beach areas where sand gets into all corners, and cleaning is difficult. A wall behind the table with shelves and a sliding door hides a small and functional bathroom, which also provides space for storage of all kitchen utensils. The large table, which serves as a dining space, makes up the kitchen and sink. The bottom part is used for storage. The large piece of furniture with the three beds runs along the wall and turns into a tall wardrobe, leaving a small space for a sofa, which can become a bed in case of emergency. In just a few square feet, a multifunctional area with plenty of free space was obtained, covering all basic needs for a short holiday break, where it is not expected visitors will spend long periods of time inside.

380 sq ft

Photographs © **Vercruisse & Dujardin/owi.bz**

Every inch of space here was thoroughly calculated to integrate all the facilities. In spite of the size of the furniture, the result is a roomy atmosphere.

Enric Rovira Apartment

Francesc Rifé

Barcelona, Spain, 2005

The renowned chocolate confectioner Enric Rovira wanted a residence that would incorporate his office and showroom. Due to the narrow and reduced dimensions of the space, the two areas were clearly defined without entirely separating them. A black granite staircase marks the entry and divides the living room from the studio. Dark floors in the entrance hall contrast with the oak floors in the rest of the apartment. The versatile and diaphanous space is characterized by chromatic contrasts between black, white, and wood. Possessing only one light source, the studio-showroom is located within an open space furnished with a central working table along with various display stands that exhibit the designs and project exquisite images of chocolate. The oak kitchen unit integrates extractable modules to accommodate a varying number of guests. A translucent glass panel transforms the living room into a private space and also offers the possibility of concealing the kitchen unit. In the bedroom, a multifunctional closet reinforces the versatile nature of the project.

750 sq ft

Photographs © **Eugeni Pons**

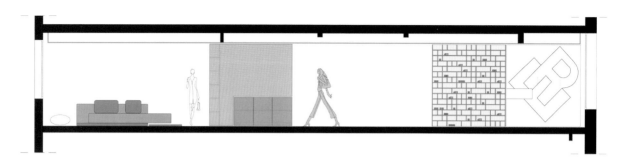

East Section

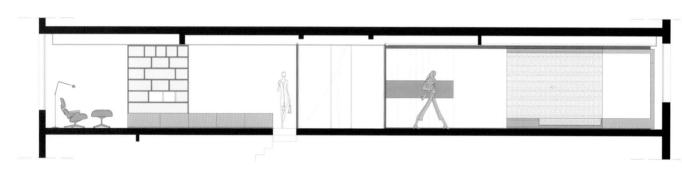

West section

0 1 2

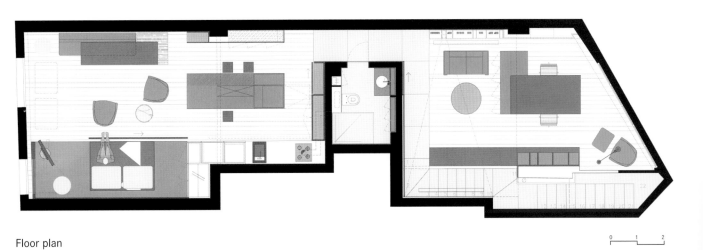

Floor plan

0   1   2

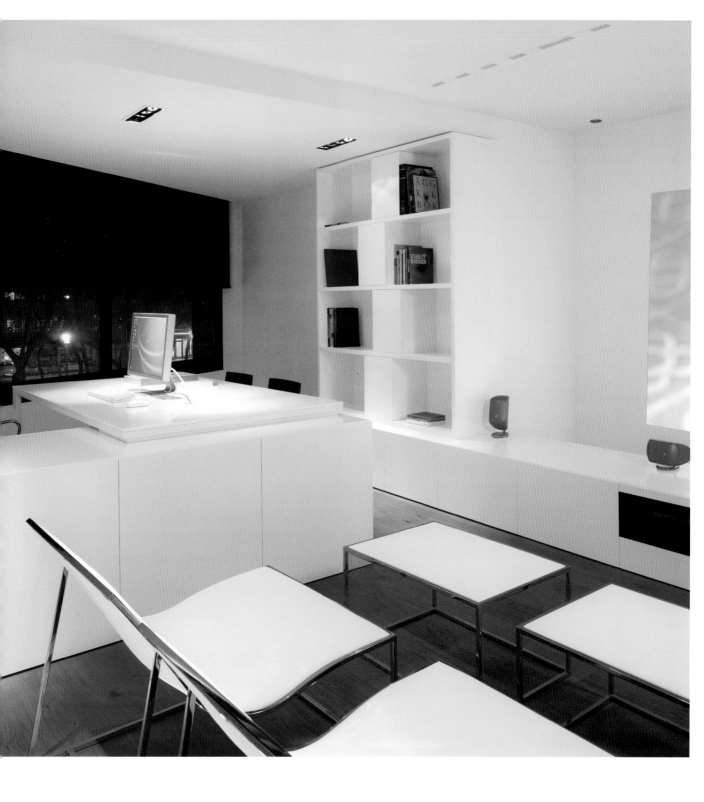

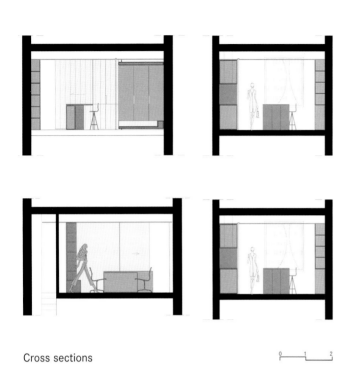

Cross sections

0   1   2

This residence that serves as a home, studio, and showroom separates the home on the left and the studio on the right using color and extractable modules. The bedroom and kitchen can be hidden by a large sliding smoked glass door.

Apartment on Rue Cadet

Marchi Architectes

Paris, France, 2005

This 320-square-foot space integrates a multitude of functions into a single environment. The kitchen unit folds inward in the blink of an eye to become a wooden wall with a rectangular opening lit from within. Opposite, another ingenious construction functions as a bed alcove that can be closed off for greater privacy. The bed is elevated onto a one-and-a-half-foot platform that incorporates storage space for clothes and personal objects. An adjacent bathroom and shower with abundant natural light can be accessed either from the bedroom or main living area. A large opening in the platform and a foldout table make for a practical studio and working space. By allowing independent functions within one single space, this minute apartment was transformed into a comfortable and multifunctional residence.

320 sq ft

Photographs © **Yasmine Eid-Sabbagh**

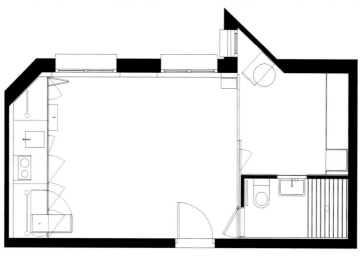

Floor plan

0   1   2

The bed is elevated on a sixteen-inch-tall platform, composed of several removable volumes, which constitute storage space. Next to this bedroom, the bathroom can be accessed from the bedroom and from the central space.

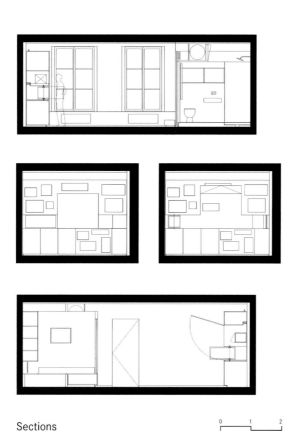

Sections

0   1   2

Apartment near the Colosseum

Filippo Bombace

Rome, Italy, 2006

750 sq ft

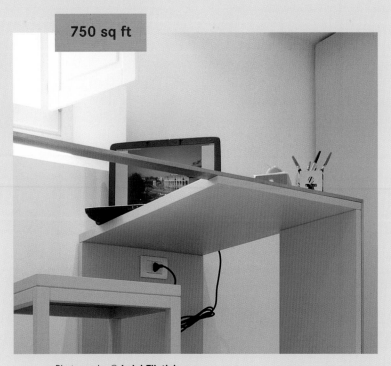

Photographs © **Luigi Filetici**

This small apartment with a privileged view of one the most emblematic structures in Europe was renovated by the architect Filippo Bombace, keeping in mind its location and the urban elements that surround it. The architect opted for colors and materials that reflect the surrounding landscape: antique green and oak reminiscent of the nearby gardens of the Caelian Hill and stone gray and purple, which adorn the mural in the living area and harmonizes with the upholstery. The living and dining rooms are linked with the kitchen by a pantry that incorporates a breakfast bar. The corridor that leads to the private areas, including the bedroom and two bathrooms, was decorated with the same color palette. In the bedroom, the bed is situated underneath a small mezzanine that holds a studio. Fabrics hung vertically were used throughout the apartment to create subtle divisions without interrupting the spacious views.

This colorful apartment reflects the green of the adjacent gardens and gray of the historic Colisseum on the opposite side. A larder connects the living area to the kitchen.

Morrell Apartment

Philip Mathieson

Sydney, Australia, 2002

645 sq ft

Photographs © **Sharrin Rees**

The Morrell apartment is situated in a privileged location of Darling Point, south of the Sydney Bay, and offers spectacular views of the ocean, port, and city. The owner needed a space to receive and accommodate guests and friends, so the renovation of the apartment included building a new bedroom while maintaining spaciousness. The living room is separated from the bedrooms by a long storage unit, which runs the entire height of the apartment and integrates an open kitchen. The sleeping areas and bathroom are located behind this unit. Mirror was used to cover surfaces in the kitchen and opposite the terrace, multiplying the space and allowing views of the exterior even when not facing that direction. Located on an angle of the building, the bedrooms open up to the exterior.

Floor plan

0 1 2

Polished, glossy surfaces dominate
all the rooms in this apartment, and
mirrors play an essential part reflecting
light and multiplying the space.

Pied à terre in Paris

Laurent Croissandeau

Paris, France, 2005

This apartment was renovated by interior designer Laurent Croissandeau for a couple that wanted a relaxing space in which to spend short periods of time. The aim of the project was to lend the residence the air of a sophisticated and cosmopolitan hotel suite. Endowed with large windows on either side, the rectangular apartment was divided in two in order to create a generously sized living room. A small bedroom leads to a dressing room, which in turn leads to the bathroom and finally to the kitchen and living room. Each area enjoys abundant natural light, creating a relaxing and tranquil atmosphere. In order to privilege the spaciousness of the living room, the dining room was located within the kitchen. Certain furniture pieces were created by the designer, such as the ebony sideboard inside the living room. All of the woodwork, including those in the living room as well as those in the private rooms, are lined with ebony to lend uniformity to the interior.

730 sq ft

Photographs © **Pierrick Bourgoin**

All the woodwork was custom-made using Macassar ebony, from the sliding doors to the wardrobes in the dressing room or the bathroom furniture, which provide great homogeneity to the entire apartment.

Floor plan

0   1   2

Day Freckman Apartment

Burley Katon Halliday

Sydney, Australia, 2006

This apartment by the Sydney Harbor has impressive views of the ocean and a profile of the city. A rectangular living room, with dining room, was designed in the part of the house that enjoys the most direct sunlight. The rest of the apartment was divided into longitudinal halves by the construction of a large module that serves as storage area while integrating the kitchen's work area and the bathroom. From the bathroom, one can watch a small television, which is incorporated into the mirror surface that is part of the central module. This whole central volume is covered in mirrors, creating an optical game and increasing the sense of space. On the opposite side, also facing this volume, is a small studio and bedroom. With bathroom and bedroom facing each other, they are easily accessible. All areas have fluid communication and can be closed with sliding doors. What makes this apartment a magnificent and radiant home is the abundance of mirrors, which reflect the light right to the end and reproduce some spaces into others. The use of white-streaked marble in the kitchen and bathroom contributes to this effect, while the floor's polished wood, cream colors, and use of soft and specific lighting throughout the apartment provide the necessary warm counterpoint.

750 sq ft

Photographs © **Sharrin Rees**

In this apartment, the use of mirrors in large surfaces magnifies all the rooms creating a genuine feeling of spaciousness.

The long central volume integrates parts of the bathroom and kitchen, so that corridors running parallel on both sides become part of the rooms, thus emphasizing the sense of openness.

Heart of Home

I 29 Office for Design

Amsterdam, Netherlands, 2004

This project's basic trait is the fact that the apartment works as a compact box, a dynamic machine in which the home develops. The design is minimal, yet very detailed. By integrating the wardrobe, bathroom, and kitchen modules, the rest of the space is available to be used freely. All the doors and covers were designed without handles to give each object a distinct feel. This house was completely emptied in order to turn it into a comfortable space consisting of one single volume, which included all the necessary areas for living. The rest of the space was furnished with Vitra and Mooi designs. The apartment was divided into three areas, leaving the front area, close to the road, for the kitchen, dining room, and meeting room. The living room and general relaxation area are in the central part, while reading and rest areas are located in the back, near the building's garden. These areas are well defined, without using any objects or furniture that obstructs the pathway, using simple materials of great quality. The floor, made of Uni Walton linoleum, is covered in a shiny rubber, which absorbs all scratches. The central volume is made of bamboo and MDF painted in white, while the bathroom surfaces are covered with an intense green epoxy.

600 sq ft

Photographs © **I 29 Office for Design**

Perspective

This volume not only integrates several functions but also creates a great amount of storage room. The remaining area of the apartment is freed by packing together those services used only few times every day.

Ponzano House

Mariano Martín

Madrid, Spain, 2003

645 sq ft

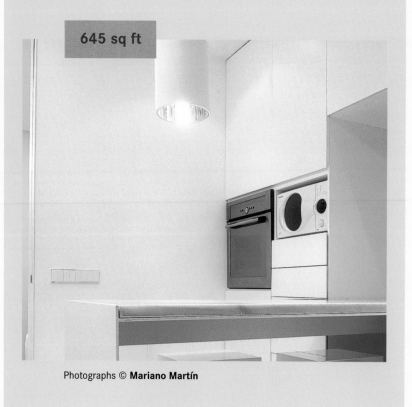

Photographs © **Mariano Martín**

The floor plan of this house located in the center of Madrid was entirely opened up to allow the natural light that enters through its two facades to reach the interior. The space was organized with an MDF structure lacquered in white that spreads out to different areas of the residence and doubles as storage space. The structure incorporates two pivoting doors that isolate the bedroom and entrance, leaving only the common spaces in view, and also integrates furniture for the kitchen and bathroom, both conceived as independent boxes. The remaining elements are concealed at the rear so that they remain out of sight from the bedroom and living room. A step marks the transition from resin to white marble floors, while full-length translucent windows diffuse light from the exterior. Sliding doors concealed within the central volume isolate these elements. In the living room, which faces the exterior, a custom-made table of white lacquered MDF contains an opal glass box lit from within to create a luminous object. At certain points within the residence, mirrors infinitely multiply the space.

The whole apartment follows the
essential concept of pure lines and
warm lighting. Therefore, custom-built
furniture was designed, such as
the coffee table that incorporates
a cubic lamp.

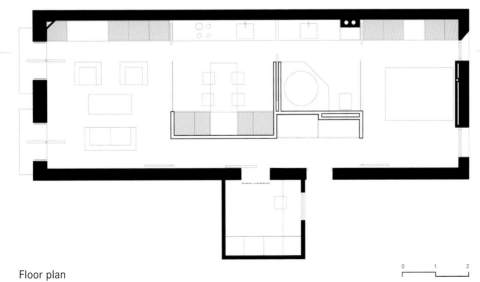

Floor plan

0   1   2

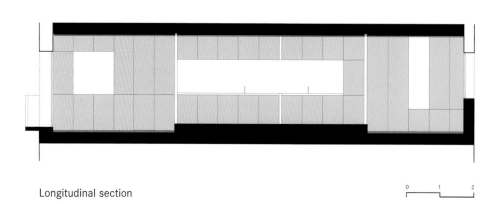

Longitudinal section

0   1   2

Mark and Avi's Apartment

David Khouri/Comma

New York, USA, 2003

592 sq ft

Photographs © **Reto Guntli/zapaimages.com**

The couple who occupied this luminous apartment decided to take a risk and renovate it according to the style that most appealed to them at the time. In an attempt to avoid following neutral and permanent formulas, as they had done previously and which had ended up boring them, they launched themselves into a highly playful design with radical combinations. Together with architect David Khouri, who was responsible for some of the rooms, they came up with a homely and cheerful space. Firstly, the floor was clad in a shiny, cobalt blue, plastic material, which offered a Mediterranean character as well as harmonizing with the shades of orange and brown that dominate the apartment.

At the end of the lounge they installed a large cupboard of Indian rose tree wood whose many compartments accommodate all types of objects and services: from stereos and books to cutlery and crockery. A lighting system was installed in the kitchen that changes colors ranging from vibrant orange to fluoride pink, and the cupboard doors are fabricated from material taken from car mudguards. At the entrance to the bedroom, on the other side of the small passageway, the doors were taken away, and the space is flanked by two large individual wardrobes.

The apartment was redesigned with the idea of becoming a playful, relaxing space. Many elements were given a special touch, such as the illuminated glass closet in the hallway.

TRANSPORTABLE
SOLUTIONS

Nomad Home

Hobby A. & Gerold Peham

Salzburg, Austria, 2005

237-948 sq ft

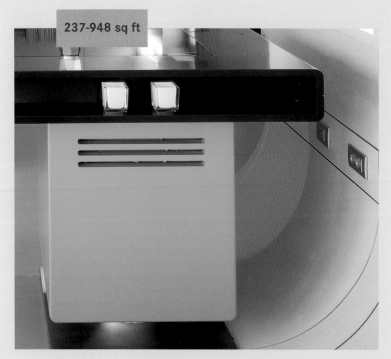

Photographs © **Angelo Kaunat**

The Nomad Home modules originated from an idea by Gerold Peham of a box-shaped transportable home. The objective was to live in nature without being tied down to any specific place. For this, the modules can be unassembled into individual pieces and assembled anywhere one wishes. Starting from a basic structure, modules of different surfaces area can be created. The same designer lives and works in one of these portable homes and changes location with the help of a truck.

The curved steel structure forms a volume eight feet tall that includes all the water and electric installations services for initial expandable modules. The walls can be interchanged for opaque or transparent glass panels, as desired. Not only can the size of the Nomad Home change but also its distribution can be structured according to different needs. One of the proposals functions with solar energy, a water deposit, and purifier. Given that the Nomad Home does not require foundations, it can be easily installed in parking lots, roof tops, or any other land plot. The metal covering of the exterior is completed with birch wood boards that form a terrace.

An opening in the covering functions as a heating or ventilation system depending on the season. Aluminum plates protect the windows from the excess light, when necessary.

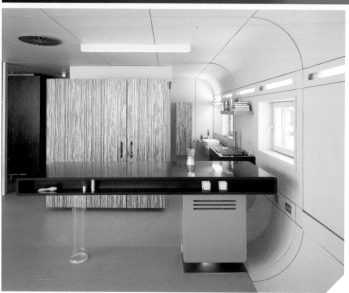

Starting from a basic structure, it is possible to assemble modules with different sizes. Materials were chosen on the basis of their stability and durability.

Self-sufficient Modules

Cannatà & Fernandes Arquitectos

Abrantes, Portugal, 2003

Commissioned by CAPA and DST, C&F architects built two prototypes of so-called Self-sufficient Modules for the Concreta Fair. They wanted to address a variety of functions by using modules that could provide the answer to the needs of temporary housing, such as an environmental observatory, surveillance posts, bars, and kiosk. The proposal included a type of module with adjustable functions, which, at the same time could be reproduced endlessly, thus being able to create instant areas or estates without causing an environmental impact and allowing construction in restricted areas. The lightness of the construction materials means they can be transported by truck or helicopter. In addition to responding to new ways of using space, each module or container also attempts to be open to the use of technology, allowing greater energy control. Photovoltaic panels make independent energy production systems possible. The modules' humid parts are sustained individually through a prefabricated water tank. A vacuum sewer system deals with the drainage of sewage water. Mechanical systems are supported by a photovoltaic panel and chargeable batteries for artificial light and electrical appliances.

290 sq ft

Photographs © **Cannatà & Fernandes Arquitectos**

The modules are designed to respond to high demands of comfort and their operation is based on sustainable processes, using solar panels and applying high-tech devices.

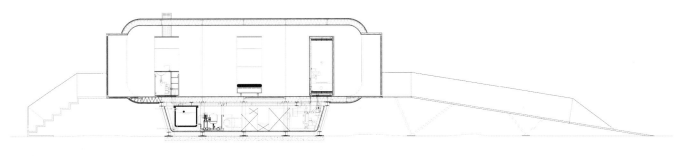

Section

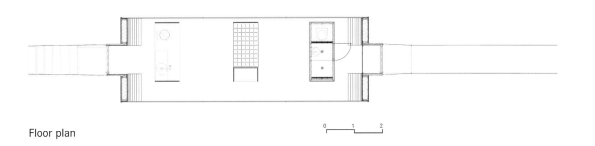

Floor plan

0   1   2

Loftcube

Werner Aisslinger/Studio Aisslinger

Berlin, Germany, 2004

Loftcube is a prefabricated mobile living unit, with a variety of design and construction possibilities, including a combination of different materials for the walls, such as transparent and translucent glass or strips of wood for ventilation. Loftcube can be set up anywhere, from the top of a building to a piece of land or a garden. Inside, the divisions of areas can also be transformed by the floor rails, which allow dividing panels to move and create different areas. These homes are divided into nighttime and daytime areas, bathroom, and kitchen. Divisions are created with Corian panels, with double functions. For example, the panel separating the kitchen and the bathroom has an integrated faucet, which can be used on both sides serving the bathroom and kitchen sinks. Similarly, the showerhead in the panel that separates the living room from the bathroom can also be used to water the small interior garden located just behind the panel. Corian was used in the kitchen area to build the stove unit. Being durable, uniform, and easily thermo-molded, this material is ideal for a space where flexibility is required.

420 sq ft

Photographs © **Steffen Jänicke**

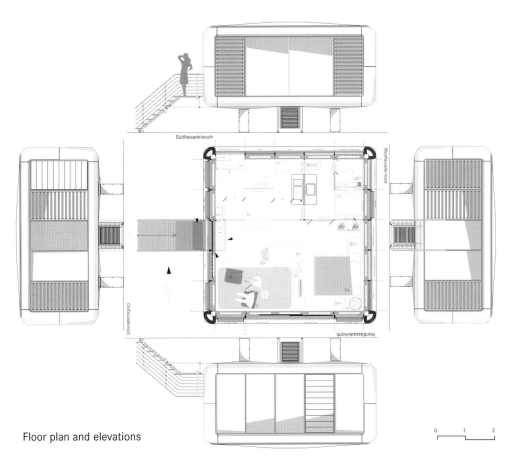

Südfassade/south

Westfassade/west

Ostfassade/east

Nordfassade/north

Floor plan and elevations

0   1   2

Inside, the space can be subdivided
with sliding panels or tracks. The
double-sided panels form the living
space onto which all portable furniture
modules are attached.

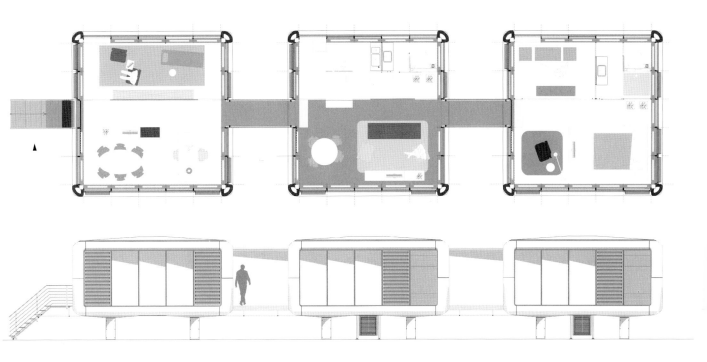

Floor plans and elevations

0 1 2

Intelligent House

Cannatà & Fernandes Arquitectos

Matosinhos, Portugal, 2002

This modular apartment, which has received numerous awards and press coverage since its completion, presents a sustainable architectural design based on domotics and suggests an optimistic solution for the immediate future, where problems of space and the price of land raise questions about the current dynamic of housing conception and construction. Technological advances open doors for architects who seek innovation in the area of new types of homes that are adaptable to different places and offer flexible interiors. An attractive exterior and a comfortable interior can reflect ideas of simplicity, flexibility, and sustainability. Today's family needs flexible, easily convertible spaces, where privacy can be obtained without walls and without having to close any doors. Similarly, this sense of space needs to be possible without having to knock down walls. The construction materials must be minimal and meet a contemporary person's comfort, hygiene, aesthetic, durability, and maintenance needs. This house proposes a revolution in the construction process, reducing the number of workers as well as its construction time, thanks to the increase in flexibility and the integration of numerous prefabricated elements. The project is based on active, rather than passive, energy saving, self-sufficient equipment, and the creation of clean air, with humidity and temperature conditions suitable to environmental comfort.

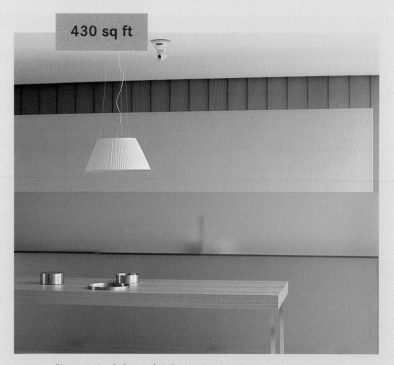

430 sq ft

Photographs © **Cannatà & Fernandes Arquitectos**

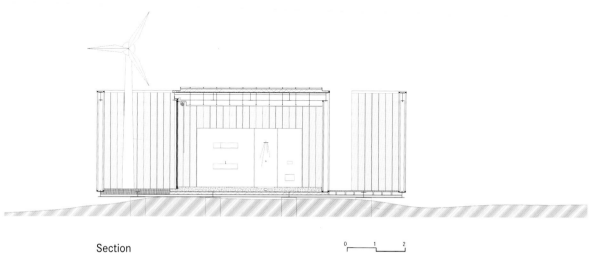

Section

0 1 2

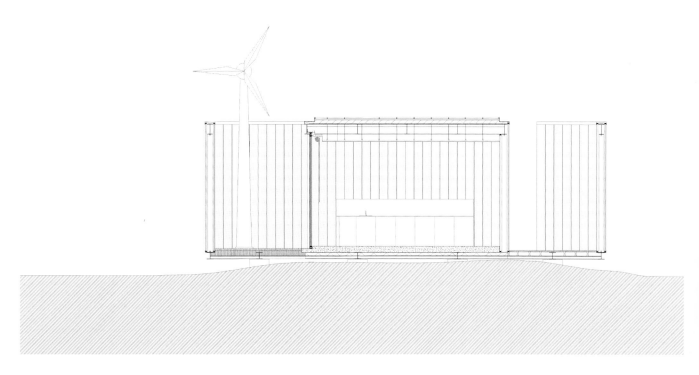

Section

Clear-cut lines, simple materials, and polished surfaces are the main formal features of a concept intended to be built and dismantled in an easy and affordable way.